By the same author

Travel and general books:

THEY DIDN'T MEAN TO KILL
LET'S LOOK AT AMERICA
ROUND THE WORLD IN 465 DAYS
OPTIMISTS IN AFRICA
GOOD, GOD AND MAN

Mystery stories including those about Roger West, Gideon, The Toff, The Baron, Dr. Palfrey, Dr. Cellini and Patrick Dawlish.

# EVOLUTION TO DEMOCRACY

John Creasey's political activities began in South West London at the age of twelve, when he first began to work for the Liberal Party in the belief that Liberals would govern on behalf of all the people; not for just one group or faction. Forty years later, he was convinced beyond doubt that if democracy in Britain were even to survive, a radical change in our parliamentary system was imperative: government by any single party was simply dictatorship masquerading as democracy.

For fifty years, even so-called 'sweeping victories' at General Elections had in fact given absolute power to parties which had actually received a *minority* of the votes cast; that is, more people had voted *against* the new government than *for* it. The gravely undemocratic aspect of this situation was obviously unrecognised by the great majority of voters, who were as obviously unaware of the utter powerlessness of the Opposition under our present system. Not once in over a hundred years, for instance, has an Opposition defeated a Government Bill!

Such a system, John Creasey concluded, *must* be abolished; for under it, no government could ever have the support of all the people. It was no use calling for the abolition of one system of government, however, without offering an unarguably better alternative. In his search for that alternative, he evolved *All Party Alliance*: a system which not only guarantees the true representative government which is ours by right, but, while ensuring a strong, *effective* Opposition, safeguards both the political identity of each party and the democratic rights of every individual.

*All Party Alliance* is based on the obvious truth that there are men of great ability, valuable experience, wisdom, and high ideals in every party—and on the firm belief that our system of government should allow the best men of all the parties to work together for the good of Britain.

In this book, the author submits that his case for *All Party Alliance* is proven. He also shows how (through *Alliance in Industry*) industrial as well as political and social justice can be absolutely ensured. And he argues that this and this alone can bring the unity of purpose which the nation must achieve if it is ever to recover economic prosperity.

In his opening chapter, he tells the impressive story of his spirited fight to establish *All Party Alliance* as a national movement with—as it is today—ever-increasing public support. And in her summation of its progressive influence and long-term impact, Olga Stringfellow tells much that is vivid, vital and warmly human of John Creasey himself, the movement's founder.

# EVOLUTION TO DEMOCRACY

## by

# John Creasey

With a summation by

OLGA STRINGFELLOW

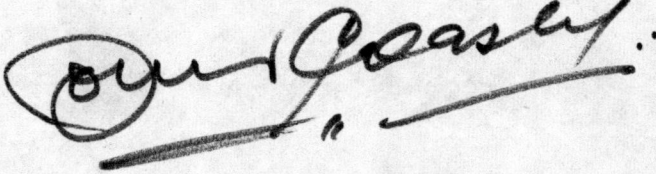

**HODDER AND STOUGHTON**

PRINTED IN GREAT BRITAIN FOR HODDER AND STOUGHTON LIMITED,
ST. PAUL'S HOUSE, WARWICK LANE, LONDON, E.C.4
BY COMPTON PRINTING LTD, LONDON AND AYLESBURY

"I am not an advocate for frequent changes in laws and constitutions. But laws and institutions must go hand in hand with the progress of the human mind. As that becomes more developed, more enlightened, as new discoveries are made, new truths disclosed, and manners and opinions change with the change of circumstances, institutions must advance also to keep pace with the times . . .

"Nothing is unchangeable, but the inherent and unalienable rights of man."

Thomas Jefferson.

# CONTENTS

Page

# THE HOW AND WHY

of

## All Party Alliance

| YEAR | WINNING PARTY | TOTAL VOTE *FOR* | TOTAL VOTE *AGAINST* | *ANTI-GOVERNMENT ELECTORAL* MAJORITY | GOVERNMENT 'MAJORITY' (SEATS IN HOUSE) |
|------|---------------|------------------|----------------------|--------------------------------------|-----------------------------------------|
| 1945 | Labour        | 11,985,733       | 13,032,660           | 1,046,927                            | 146                                     |
| 1950 | Conservative  | 13,265,610       | 15,503,967           | 2,238,357                            | 8                                       |
| 1951 | Conservative  | 13,718,069       | 14,878,626           | 1,160,557                            | 26                                      |
| 1955 | Conservative  | 13,311,938       | 13,448,816           | 136,878                              | 59                                      |
| 1959 | Conservative  | 13,750,965       | 14,112,373           | 361,408                              | 100                                     |
| 1964 | Labour        | 12,205,181       | 15,450,568           | 3,245,387                            | 5                                       |
| 1966 | Labour        | 13,064,951       | 14,198,655           | 1,133,704                            | 99                                      |

# 1

My political activities began in South-West London at the age of twelve, when I first started to work for the Liberal Party. I was told, and believed, that Liberals would govern on behalf of all the people, not just one group or faction. Forty years later, experience brought me to the conclusion that no one party could ever do this. I became convinced beyond doubt that if democracy in Britain was even to survive, a radical change in our parliamentary system was imperative: one-party government could no longer be tolerated or excused.

I believe that government by *any* single party must be abolished, for four different reasons:

1. Because a government drawn from members of a single party represents only those who voted at the relevant General Election *for* that party. Those who voted *against* the winning party may be represented in Parliament: they are *never* represented in the government itself. Their voice can be heard only in an Opposition which, being unable to defeat a government-sponsored Bill during the life of any Parliament, is totally impotent to *act* on their behalf: a so-called 'democratic watchdog' which is all bark and no bite.

2. Because *all* British governments since the Second World War have been elected by a *minority* of those who voted: that is, more people voted *against* the new government than for it. Yet each of the seven different governments (4 Labour, 3 Conservative) had absolute power during its term of office. Even if democracy is defined simply as 'majority rule', this is a travesty of democratic justice.

3. Because, as we can see from the above, our present system leads inevitably to government by dictatorship, masquerading as democracy. Since, under our present system, the Opposition *cannot* defeat a government-sponsored Bill, even a party with a tiny majority in the House of Commons can and does do exactly what it wants *against the wishes of a majority of the electorate.* No government Bill has been defeated by the Opposition in over a hundred years. What government defeats there have been, were always the result of revolt within the ruling party itself.

4. Because government by any single party automatically divides the nation into two opposing camps—the pro-government and the anti-government—making unity of purpose and endeavour impossible.

Awareness of the divisive elements in British politics came very early, for me. I had joined the Liberal Party when it was being torn apart by the Lloyd George-Asquith feud, from which it has never recovered, so I cut my political teeth on the sterility and the dangers of disunity.

That lesson was promptly and sharply driven home as the great miners' strike of 1921 split the British people into hostile camps. Half a decade later, during the General Strike of 1926, I saw in the streets of London the hunger marches, the soup kitchens, the cars wrecked and burned: all the tragic ugliness of internecine strife, as Englishman turned on Englishman, Welshman on Welshman, Scot on Scot. The government called out the Army to support the police, and university students and hosts of white-collar workers flung themselves into a bitter fight against the strikers.

As the years passed, I learned of and sympathised with the sincere motives of all the groups involved; but at the time, it seemed to me that the country was being ravaged by a kind of civil war between two sides seeking power. I could only look on, anguished that men could be so blind to their fundamental identity of interest; their unavoidable inter-dependence. No one seemed to realise this truth, least of all the parties of the Left and Right, who ranged themselves behind the embattled factions, making political capital out of national tragedy.

These were the days of the dreadful 'depression'. When I was nearly eighteen, and had been working for three years, I lost what had seemed a good job for life, and in the next nine years was to be out of work far more often that I was in. In all, I had twenty-five jobs and was sacked twenty-four times—often, as happened to so many in those days, at only an hour's notice. (I left the last job in 1935, to start writing for a living, safe in the certainty that I could earn at least two pounds per week.)

Everywhere I looked, at eighteen, people were out of work, often three millions at a time. As I tried to do my share in countering the appalling effects of the Conservative v. Socialist class war, which Liberals at least recognised for what it was, it seemed to me even more and more certain that the only form of government which could end the tragic mess was one which

could unite, not divide the people. Still convinced that
Liberals alone were capable of bridging the widening chasm
and forging any kind of unity, I worked unceasingly for the
party. Fly-posting ... pushing leaflets through letter-boxes
... addressing envelopes ... organising wards ... speaking at
meetings—I did them all. In 1945, I acted as the Liberal
candidate's agent at Bournemouth, repeated this in a
by-election a few months later, and in 1950 fought the seat
myself, getting 9,216 votes: one of the largest Liberal polls in
the country. I was a member of the Liberal Party Council in
the days when Lord Beveridge's National Health proposals
were adopted and improved, when the policy of co-ownership
was formulated, and the strength of Liberal policy made hopes
of a Liberal revival run high.

These hopes were dashed at one General Election after
another. Slowly, a disturbing change overcame the Party.
Many of its most able members went to the Right or Left, or
out of politics altogether. Instead of basing policies on the
democratic rights of all the people, those who remained in the
Party began to base them on the interests of one particular
section of the populace—Liberals, radicals, reformers; whatever
name they chose.

Conservative governments unashamedly submitted the
whole nation to Conservative policies. Labour governments
unashamedly submitted the whole nation to Socialist policies.
Communists and Fascists would assuredly submit us all to
Communist or Fascist policies, given half a chance. And now,
Liberals wanted to inflict solely Liberal policies on a far from
solely Liberal electorate.

The fact that the policies I believed in would prosper from
a Liberal victory did not alter the fact that Liberal philosophy
was in stark contradiction to my belief that as it takes all sorts

to make a nation, every government should govern in the interests of all and at the will of all the people. I had fought all my life against parties which governed in the interests of one group—and thus, of necessity, against the interests of others. Now, even the party in which I had placed such faith was prepared, if the chance ever came, to perpetuate that wholly unjust and plainly discredited system.

As the Liberal leaders moved away from what I held, and still hold, to be true Liberalism, the younger members becoming more and more militantly Left-wing, more and more obsessed with 'power', more and more intolerant of other views than their own, I resigned from the Party.

It was meant to be 'retirement': I was leaving politics for good, and not without relief. It had cost a great deal of time and money and, while I had managed to build up a world-wide public for my books, it had meant that all my writing (and what also 'fed' the writing: my travelling) was done at very great pressure.

I longed for leisure, and secretly felt that I had earned it. The long weary years of political battling, after all, had been spent on behalf of others: as a writer, it made little or no difference to my personal fortunes what party governed the nation. I could go where I liked, live where I chose, and in far greater comfort than most. The time had come to concentrate on my own interests: I would take a long trip around the globe, visiting all my overseas editors and publishers.

During this period, Britain was even more bitterly divided than usual, politically. Her industry was bedevilled by strikes, her economy was going down and down and her taxes up and up. Yet here was I, essentially a 'political animal' from boyhood, telling myself that I did not care: that I had done more than my share. That politics was a 'dirty business', and that I could be better off without involvement in it.

The truth, of course, was that my disillusion with the Liberal Party had gone very deep. Too deep to listen yet to the still, small voice which protested that turning my back on a dirty business would do nothing towards cleaning it up . . .

In 1962, I set off with my family on a round-the-world trip planned to last eighteen months.

I had made one previous world tour, twelve years before, for the express purpose of finding new markets and fresh backgrounds for my books. It had been a great success, financially, and also a wonderful opportunity to meet the peoples and study, at first hand, the social, political and industrial scenes of other nations. On that first trip, I had found the name of Britain—coupled with that of Winston Churchill—greatly respected and very often revered, in every country I visited.

Between that first world trip and the second, moreover, I had visited most of the Iron Curtain countries. Once I drove through West and East Germany, Poland and Russia to Moscow, in a Bentley which, wherever I stopped, drew crowds who gazed in open admiration at this impressive example of British craftsmanship.

My second world tour was at least as personally successful as the first. But the change of attitude towards Britain which I encountered everywhere was indescribable.

Far from being revered and respected, we were variously pitied, derided, and despised. Everywhere, I met the same sort of criticisms: "You have built a Welfare State on money borrowed from us." "You don't pay your debts." "You don't put your backs into your work." "The quality of your products has fallen right off: a dozen countries can sell us better stuff today—*and* guarantee delivery dates!"

I hated, and deeply resented, this sweeping and arbitrary condemnation; yet I had to examine it closely, for there could well be truth in it.

The world's memory is short, of course. Erstwhile enemy and erstwhile ally alike either do not remember, or choose to forget, that what caused us to get so heavily into debt in the first place was the cost of two world wars fought at great sacrifice—to save our own lives, it is true; but also, just as truly, to save freedom. We had been left on our own to fight, and largely to pay for the early years of this war. Even the United States stayed virtually aloof while Hitler rampaged over and ravaged all Europe—until at last the Japanese attack at Pearl Harbour brought home the urgent danger.

Until Pearl Harbour, our help from the United States was largely by Lend-Lease, a system of 'buy-now-and-pay-later'. Under this system, as well as food and raw materials, we obtained weapons which were, sadly, often obsolete. Because of the bitter hostility to the United States entering the war Lend-Lease was America's only help to a nation fighting a desperate battle to stem a hideous tide which could sweep away all the principles of freedom which Jefferson and Lincoln had so vividly expressed, and in which countless Americans believed so passionately.*

Once America was 'in', of course, Lend-Lease was enormously increased, and was wholly vital to victory in Europe. But the fact remains that in the end—with British industry either destroyed or nearly obsolete, our financial and economic resources virtually exhausted—the Truman administration cut off all supplies of Lend-Lease with one ruthless stroke, on the very day the war with Europe ended!

It is true that such a decapitation had been written into the

*Yet Great Britain still repays capital and pays interest on these debts.

17

Lend-Lease Act by Congress and that, by legislation, President Truman had no choice. Nevertheless the severance cut into the very vitals of a nation which had given everything, unstintingly, to fight a war without which the free world could not have been saved. Moreover, successive American governments thereafter treated Great Britain with far less generosity—and even less simple fairness—than they treated their defeated enemies. I have long been convinced that this was largely due to Big Business interests determined to take over British markets while Britain was too exhausted to prevent it.

Whatever else had contributed to Britain's obvious plight and resultant loss of world prestige, however, I was sure that the major cause lay in the inherently divisive, socially unjust and economically impracticable political and industrial system which the nation had outgrown— and which a rising generation found totally unacceptable. I was as sure that while this outworn system kept the nation bitterly divided, party politicians, Trade Union leaders and industrialists, either from blind prejudice or blind ignorance, did everything they possibly could to make sure it stayed that way.

The more countries I visited, the more criticism I heard. And the greater my opportunity to see Britain dispassionately from afar, the more positive I became that if we were ever to pull ourselves out of the mire, the nation must be united. The only question was: How?

Clearly there had to be an answer: some way of creating both political and industrial unity at home. Just as clearly, no such unity could ever be possible under a system which so flagrantly denied even simple political justice to more than half the nation, whichever party was in power.

There had to be really effective reform; and reform

demonstrably in the interests of all the nation—radical, but not disruptive; evolution, but not revolution. Obviously the prime need was for a formula which would guarantee to provide an absolutely truly representative government, already ours by constitutional right, but automatically denied us under the present 'two-party' system of alternating one-party rule.

Back in England I drew up, stage by stage, two sets of proposals which I believed would, together, lead to true democracy. They were based, very simply, on the instinctive need for human justice. One, the political, I called *All Party Alliance,* the other, *Alliance in Industry.*

Quite confident that these proposals offered at least the fundamental basis of a new system, I submitted them to various leaders of the Liberal Party. I confess I had great hopes. After all, mine were the kind of socially progressive proposals that Liberals of my early days would have openly acclaimed, developed in great detail, and fought for tooth and nail.

I was quickly disillusioned again, meeting derision from some, cold disinterest from others, and from a few a grudging acknowledgement that the concept might one day be practicable. But in none was there any sign of readiness to relinquish personal dreams of Liberal government and Liberal power. Most, indeed, would not even study these proposals for a system which they knew I claimed would give the millions of Liberal electors in this country the voice in their own government that has been denied them for fifty years.

I went, in turn, to members of the Conservative and Labour parties.

"Don't waste your time," all of them said. "If you want to come back into politics, join us."

I next took the proposals to the national Press, finding of

course that newspapers, too, have their party allegiances—and pressures—and the cold wall of indifference met me wherever I went.

I had either to give up, or change my method of attack.

Pulling out, at that stage, was tempting indeed. I was more disillusioned than ever with politics and politicians, while I had spent nearly two years in fruitless endeavour. I contemplated giving up very seriously and only one fact stopped me: that the people, the electors, had no knowledge of *All Party Alliance,* and in a democracy only the people can be the final arbiters. I felt sure that once they had been informed and had had time to digest the proposed new system, they would demand that the parties adopt it. The *need* for a system that voters of all parties could truly respect was—as it still is—so very obvious.

Millions of men and women, at every General Election, either abstained from voting or openly admitted to voting not from conviction but 'for the lesser of two evils' or 'to keep the others out'. Moreover, at this time, many more millions of convinced party voters were feeling the ache of disillusion and were very sensitive to the repeated failures of successive governments, no matter of which party. I was sure that the vast majority of electors would heartily welcome a system which would give real purpose to every election: real value to every vote.

The question was: how to reach them? How to convince them that *All Party Alliance* would achieve these things?

Nation-wide advertising campaigns can be afforded by the parties, out of their solid financial backing—of Conservatism by big business; of Socialism, by the Trade Unions. Anything I spent had to come out of my own pocket. So I could not even begin to afford to campaign direct to the public. The next best thing would obviously be to concentrate on putting the proposals over to those who could reach the public: the leaders of opinion, formulators of policy, setters of example, to whom the nation's interests must presumably be of paramount concern.

Even a monthly news-letter to such people would be a full-time project, however, and a very tight writing/travelling/speaking schedule for months ahead made it out of the question; I had to maintain the work schedule so as to earn the money to pay for the politics, and could not afford the expense of highly professional staff.

Throughout all these endeavours, I had been greatly helped and encouraged by Olga Stringfellow. An exceptionally able and politically-aware journalist-turned-author, she had written a best-seller in her first work of fiction, had followed it with another, and was currently at work on what promised to be a third. The first person to whom I had outlined the *All Party Alliance* proposals, she had been instantly aware of their full potential.

As deeply disturbed as I by the increasingly undemocratic state of the nation, she shared my belief that these proposals need only be made generally known to win nation-wide support. But she feared the parties would be equally swift to recognise their potential popularity and guessed each would claim (as each eventually did) that the other side would never co-operate or that the idea was hopelessly idealistic. Indeed, she was bleakly convinced that each party would do everything in its power to keep all knowledge of the proposals from the voting public.

Knowing that many of the Fleet Street initiate shared her concern, she had, however, been more optimistic than I of national newspaper approval and help. Deeply disappointed when the Press proved equally unready even to give the public a chance to judge for themselves, she offered to drop her own work for a year, and help in any way that she possibly could. So, all thought of giving up vanished. In the early spring of 1966, we began to hammer away at leaders of industry and commerce, Trade Unions and education, religion and the law, at the provincial as well as the national Press, the broadcasting networks, and every Member of Parliament . . .

The purpose of each approach was exactly the same; only the method of attack differed. We set out to convince everyone involved of the inadequacy of the present system; of our belief that the system itself created most of the evils which arose in it. That there was no hope for Britain's economy unless the nation was united; that unity was only possible with a change of system; that we were heading fast towards a form of dictatorship; that we allowed the party leaders to place their members under threat of expulsion if they dared to vote according to their conscience instead of to the dictates of their party. From time to time glaring examples arose from the parliamentary or social establishment proving how right our beliefs were; and by letters and telegrams to the Prime Minister and Leader of the Opposition, to countless others in industry, commerce, the Church and the law, we mounted a year-long campaign.

Evidence that our efforts were bearing fruit was soon forthcoming. Gradually, the less submissive M.P.s, for instance, began to rebel, to stand on their *right* to vote as conscience demanded, or at least to abstain without being thrown out of the party for their honesty. Various aspects of *All Party Alliance* policy were advocated—none of those who adopted them realising that only if the whole set of proposals were put into effect could the new system be effective: that to try to apply them one by one—to abolish Party Whips, for instance, without changing the whole system—would be simply another futile attempt to make the present system work.

However, the straws in the wind were welcome, indicating at least a change of mood. Two Fleet Street editors who opened their columns to this new concept, played a significant part in getting the A.P.A. ball rolling—in the *Sunday Times* and in the *Evening News*. For a long time, however, these proved to be exceptions to the general rule that the ideas would not be of interest to the public. Time and time again, top newspapermen who interviewed me went back to their editors filled with eager conviction that this was what the public were seeking. And time and time again, the interview was either not published, or was cut to ribbons. Editorial policy, whether inclined to the Left or Right, was adamant against putting my proposals for *All Party Alliance* before the people and allowing them to judge for themselves.

Yet the only criticism ever made by any politician, political journalist or economist has been: "It will never work, human nature being what it is."

What they failed to understand was that the very basis of *All Party Alliance* and *Alliance in Industry* lies in satisfying the instinctive demand of human nature for fair play: both new systems lies in their demonstrable ability to ensure justice and fair play to *all*, whereas the existing system can only benefit some at the expense of others.

A few editors sent their top feature writers and economists to discuss the proposals, and on countless occasions I invited them to fault any single one. Since none ever did—although several tried—it is reasonable to suppose they could not.

The truth is that no writer, no expert in any field, has ever been able to put a finger on any fallacy in the proposals. Some who thought they had found one had simply made the elementary mistake of judging the proposals in the light of the *existing* parliamentary system. They had given no thought to the vastly greater tolerance and mutual respect the new system would create between *men of all parties elected in the knowledge that their votes would have EQUAL VALUE, their judgement EQUAL weight, in the government of the nation*—whichever party held the balance of power in the House. Apart from the *London Evening News*, no single paper made the slightest attempt even to try to explain how I claimed that *All Party Alliance* would work. Yet day after day they were belabouring the parties and demanding a new and vital approach to politics.

Whatever the reason, in that first year it was all too clear that our approach to those who helped form public opinion, too, had failed as signally as the attempts to arouse the interest and concern of the parties and the politicians.

There was only one method of attack left to me: to go over the heads of the parties, over the heads of the Press, and appeal direct to the people. For anyone but a millionaire, that meant only one thing: contesting a by-election. As an old campaigner, I knew the blood and sweat and the cost of electioneering. I knew that even compared with the Liberals, who had only one-tenth of the organisation facilities of either of the other parties, an independent would fight almost insuperable odds. And I knew that political expenses not being tax-allowable, every penny spent would have to come out of what I had left after paying income and surtax.

I knew, too, that to organise and prepare for even a three-week campaign in advance of the election itself would demand in time and energy at least as much as I would expend on three or four books. Travel would have to go, luxuries would have to go, leisure would have to go.

With all three massive party-machines ranged against me, there was obviously no real hope of winning a seat. All that time, that energy, that money, would be expended to one end only: to publicise the proposals of *All Party Alliance*, to give the people at least some chance of learning that an alternative to our increasingly-discredited present system did exist.

The point of no return came one September day in 1966 when I stood in Smith Square, Westminster. On one corner was mammoth Transport House, the Headquarters of the Socialist Party; on another, the even bigger Conservative Central Office, the Tory headquarters; on a third was the then headquarters of the Liberal Party organisation.

I remember looking up, and feeling very, very small and insignificant. Dwarfed. And I remember saying, aloud: "Well, there isn't any choice. I've got to do it."

There was only one way left of showing the country the alternative to the system which was ruining the nation and prostituting democracy: by fighting a by-election which would arouse great public interest. Only thus could I hope to tell the public exactly what I believed: that with *All Party Alliance* and *Alliance in Industry* we could rid ourselves of the corruption, the self-interest, the inequalities inherent in our present system. That here was a way to run Britain at a profit; a way to bring down taxation; a way to ensure that the best brains and talents and experience from all parties could work together for the good of Britain; a way to strengthen each party's political integrity, yet make them stop their petty bickering and point-scoring and put the nation's interests first; a way to give the Opposition the power to actually defeat a bad Bill, not merely protest at it—a way to defeat it, moreover, without bringing down the government and so provoking an economic crisis.

*There was no other way to show my absolute faith that here was a means of ensuring that personal integrity in public office could replace party self-interest and political expedience: a way to make honesty LITERALLY the best policy, even in politics.*

Somehow, I had to show why I was so convinced that no one party could ever win the confidence of all the people and so unify the nation, but that the achievement of such unity was not only practicable but essential. And I had to show why I was so sure that no existing form of ownership and control of industry could possibly save the nation. Further, I had to show that I believed the present system was at the root of all our troubles because it brought out the worst in worker, management and capitalist alike. Until *all* concerned knew beyond question that they were getting both political and industrial justice, we could not hope to bring out the best in any of them.

And so I prepared for a fight.

With the resignation in late 1966 of Frank Cousins, stormy petrel of the Trade Union Movement, the strong Labour seat of Nuneaton became vacant. I decided to contest it, and Olga Stringfellow became my agent; I could not possibly have undertaken this without the absolute assurance of her dedicated help.

Serious door-to-door canvassing was out of the question, because of my polio leg. Yet with Olga Stringfellow as my entire 'political organisation' I was taking on the three solidly-entrenched political parties, with all the vast resources of their national party machines behind them, in an area of traditionally-rigid political demarcation and party following.

The voluntary workers who rallied round from the very

first were a heartening augury of what *All Party Alliance* could be in operation. Convinced Conservatives, Liberals and Socialists, of all ages and from all walks of life, came to offer their help. "We're sick of party politics," they said bitterly. "We need something different." So they folded election addresses and filled envelopes together, delivered leaflets together, they even drove together in a public cavalcade, proudly displaying their own party colours together with the silver ribbons and rosettes of *All Party Alliance.*

They talked together—as they worked together—in complete harmony. Each accepted and respected the basic political convictions of the others; each freely admitted the beneficial social advances for which the others' parties were responsible. All were completely united in their conviction that *only* through *All Party Alliance* could the country's leaders—of all parties—pool their wealth of experience and talent and work together in the best possible interests of the nation.

The appeal of *All Party Alliance* was often instantaneous; the welcome from the voters was very great indeed. However, I soon discovered that it was not simply a case of fighting the parties on issues of principle and policy. Once they discovered from their early canvassing reports that there was a substantial measure of pro-A.P.A. feeling, they set out in their time-honoured way to discredit and to smear both me and the concept of a new system. "Creasey's just out for the publicity," their canvassers would say. "He's made his money out of writing, this is just a rich man's fancy." Or, from Conservatives: "Of course, this is back-door Communism," and from Socialists: "This is Fascism in disguise."

I do not recall a single instance in which any of my opponents answered a single question about *All Party Alliance.*

Months later I learned that two of the other three candidates had never troubled to find out what I was proposing, yet on platform after platform they dismissed A.P.A. as impracticable or as hopeless idealism, while their canvassers were spreading distortions and deliberate falsehoods.

I had been in politics too long to be really surprised, but all of this made me more and more stubborn and determined.

Many of my supporters were battling against daily jeers and insults for daring to show my window-bills in party-stronghold areas—but, bless them, most stood their ground. Whilst time after time, strangers sought us out to apologise for putting up a party poster 'to keep the peace'—and assure us that A.P.A. had *their* votes and probably those of many others in the same predicament.

It is worth noting that in an age of political heckling and often physical violence there was no heckling at any *All Party Alliance* meeting. From time to time would-be 'disrupters' of the Left or Right appeared—driven by those Socialist assurances that what I proposed was simply 'back-door Fascism' or Conservative assurances that what I proposed was simply 'back-door Communism'. But without a single exception their belligerence evaporated after their first 'challenge' had been answered; and they stayed to inquire. Many hardened party hecklers confessed that they could not fault the logic or the justice of my proposals. At one and the same meeting a Conservative, a Socialist, a Liberal and a Communist started their questions in stark hostility but as the meeting progressed their questions died away, and at the end all four were eagerly advising me how to get votes from *their* party!

All of this, it is significant to note, was despite the fact that there could hardly have been a tougher constituency in which to put over a completely new concept of government. Nuneaton was a town with a stolidly-fixed, Them *v.* Us, 'my-party-right-or-wrong' approach to politics—where each side said of the other: "You could put up a donkey as their candidate, and as long as it had their colours round its neck, they'd vote for it!"

It soon became obvious, moreover, that I was labouring under one unanticipated but very grave handicap: for the most part the national Press totally ignored my campaign, while constantly keeping the other candidates (and their parties) in the public eye. It was tantamount to telling Nuneaton electors that neither I nor the system I advocated need be taken seriously. The local Press, however, was scrupulously fair.

There is no way of telling how many votes would have been cast for *All Party Alliance* had one or two of the national newspapers reported the campaign with even reasonable objectivity. As it was, newspapermen were astounded, especially those who had not been to Nuneaton during the campaign, that with 2,755 votes I took 6.4% of the total pool, an astonishing vote for *any* Independent—and this despite the fact that, towards the end of the campaign, each of the parties had brought in hundreds, even thousands, of helpers by train and coach to help stamp out the rapidly growing sympathy and support for *All Party Alliance*. At least the press reported this, and letters of congratulation, sympathy and support came from all over the country.

In the days that followed, a constant stream of strangers called at the Nuneaton campaign office to say that if they had dreamed I could get so many votes they would have added theirs to the rest. Most of them had abstained: many had voted for what they thought the lesser of two evils. All had been caught in the spurious net of the 'wasted vote' threat—the insidious *'What can ONE man do?'* (as if every reform in this world had not *begun* with one man!) . . . the accusing *'You'll only be letting the Other Lot in'*, and all the rest. The attitude of the national press had put the final touch: what to countless voters was the salvation of their country had been presented as a hopeless cause.

In the West Midlands the Nuneaton result made all politically-minded people aware of *All Party Alliance*, however. Television programmes, announcing the result, gave *All Party Alliance* its first national hearing. There had not been the break-through for which my supporters and I had so desperately hoped, but there *was* a dent in the wall of vested interests thrown up to 'the system'.

Just before the Nuneaton poll I had been forced, reluctantly, to face another issue. A second seat in the Midlands had fallen vacant: Brierley Hill, one of the largest constituencies in the country, with over 86,000 on the electoral roll. I was exhausted; so was Olga. But we were convinced that if I fought again within a few weeks of Nuneaton, no one would think I was doing it 'for fun', while I might well consolidate the advantages already gained.

So, on the night of the declaration of the poll at Nuneaton, I announced that I would fight Brierley Hill. The next day, Olga and I were in the constituency. We had just two weeks in which to prepare. I fought that campaign virtually single-handed from a caravan on a piece of wasteland, while Olga was making the round trip from Nuneaton twice daily, ferrying mailbags full of election addresses and A.P.A. literature. Somehow we managed, with the help of a staunch little band, mostly from Nuneaton, to get fifty thousand envelopes addressed and filled in time (between 'commando'-type fly-posting forays with the hardier enthusiasts!).

Public meetings were out of the question: so was any serious canvassing. Yet despite all the odds, the *All Party Alliance* vote was 2.8% of the total—astonishingly high, in the circumstances, and to me convincing proof of deep public interest in what I was trying to do*.

The trouble, now, was to decide when to stop; even though I hadn't made the break-through, the movement was much better known. Then, soon after Brierley Hill, the Labour-held seat at Gorton (Manchester) fell vacant, and when Winston Churchill's grandson became the Conservative candidate the nation-wide interest made it an obvious place to fight. So, within a few weeks of Brierley Hill, I decided to contest Gorton. There, with Olga's unflagging help, I campaigned from an empty supermarket. Once again, Nuneaton A.P.A. supporters did Trojan work with the envelope-addressing, and a handful of local supporters, as well as some from Brierley Hill, did the folding and filling. And although even the parties themselves admitted that the prospect of a Churchill defeat had been used (with great success) to rally the wavering Tories, and the prospect of a Churchill win used (with even greater success) to rally the wavering Socialists, after little over two weeks' campaigning I won 2.6% of the poll, more than accounting for the difference between the Labour winner and the Conservative runner-up. There was no longer any room for doubt: plainly, there would always be a solid vote for *All Party Alliance*. What I now needed was a *sensational* vote.

There had been one marked advance at Gorton; the local and the national press had given A.P.A. much more attention.

*Friends of old standing, Chris and Donna Dumbell, gave me warm and generous hospitality during my Brierley Hill campaign, and one highly regarded industrialist sent me, out of the blue, a cheque for £1,500, the only substantial financial help I've been given. But for this, I really doubt whether I could have got through.

Moreover, one Fleet Street man after another came up to me after my daily Press conferences to apologise for the comparatively modest space A.P.A. had received in their columns. "I sent a long story in," they told me, their reactions varying from quiet anger to gloomy resignation. "It was cut to pieces."

These, with other political pundits, were forecasting an early by-election at Oldham West (a seat young Churchill's grandfather had once fought and lost). That was close enough to Gorton for Press, television and radio coverage of the campaign to have given *All Party Alliance* some valuable background publicity, and was an overpoweringly obvious place to make another stand. Perhaps *the* place . . .

But I had set out to fight one by-election, not *four*. Three had exhausted me and nearly exhausted my financial reserves. Olga had worked herself to a standstill. I had a solid back-log of writing to make up, plus a heavy schedule of commitments ahead, all very urgent, since I had neglected so much for so long, both here and in the U.S.A. Moreover, Olga's 'one year for A.P.A.' had already been stretched to nearer two, and her unfinished book was crying out to be written. Consequently, at the declaration of the poll at Gorton I was still undecided, although Olga simply said: "I'll go along with Oldham, if you will." The count was at Manchester's gothic Town Hall; the huge chamber was crowded, young Winston Churchill demanded a recount, and the waiting increased the tension before the result was announced.

There was an outburst of boos for the Labour winner, more for the Conservative runner-up, boos for the Liberal, and boos for the Communist, who was in fifth place—behind me. *There were no boos for All Party Alliance. There never have been.* Indeed, officials and supporters from every party have gone out of their way to congratulate me on what I am trying to do; many openly admitting that they wished it could come about, others voluntarily reporting the 'astonishingly' widespread sympathy with A.P.A. they encountered at every level in their canvassing.

So, when I was called to the microphone, I made my usual, brief "All Party Alliance is bound to win" speech. And I added simply: "Oldham—here I come!" I am told that everyone who knew anything about politics was flabbergasted. This would mean *four* by-elections in less than eighteen months, quite fantastic for an Independent with no backing and only one full-time *aide*.

We went to Oldham the following day, and the campaign was virtually begun. Soon afterwards I left for the United States on an unavoidable business trip, and Olga moved to Oldham, seeking out possible helpers and putting in the vital foundation work for an out and out attack on the parties as soon as I was able to return to this country.

From late January on, driving up whenever possible (between further American and other commitments) from my home and writing headquarters near Salisbury in Wiltshire, I managed to spend some eight weeks in the area before the Writ was finally issued in May.

Support for *All Party Alliance* had been steadily growing, and in the first days of the actual campaign, the list of voluntary helpers who 'popped in' to do what they could, whenever they could, had topped the hundred mark. Once again, they were of all ages, all walks of life—*and all parties*.

I confess that I expected more than the 3,389 votes cast for *All Party Alliance*, yet there was great cause for satisfaction. Although not a real break-through, it was to many an unbelievable result for an Independent. With over 13% of the total poll, I had nearly twice as many votes as the Liberal and for the first time I had soundly beaten a major party.

Given the money, the time, and the help in making the meaning, the unarguable justice, *and the need* of this new system clear to the electors, *All Party Alliance* could obviously win a vote that would threaten the strongest party. Given even half the massive organisation and resources available to any party candidate, an A.P.A. victory would be a real possibility.

Evidence was soon forthcoming that the Oldham vote had badly jolted the Liberal Party, and shaken the others. No party and no newspaper now had the temerity to try to dismiss *All Party Alliance* as 'nonsense'. But after that shock result, the political bias of the national press, only too evident throughout the campaign, hardened into an unmistakable determination to *'stop A.P.A.'*. Nearly every one of them did their best to play down or ignore what every one of them must have known to be an incredibly high poll for an Independent.

But what mattered was that *3,389* men and women had seen a gleam of hope for political sanity and justice, and gone out to vote for it—despite the press and despite the pressures and the haranguing of the parties. Everywhere I went then—everywhere I go now—the mood of the people could be summed up as: "If only this *could* be brought about, what a wonderful thing it would be!"

I am convinced that it *will* be brought about. The hopeless failure of our present system becomes increasingly self-evident. In fact, the need for a system of government which will unite the nation in common cause, and inspire real confidence in the nation's leadership, is fast becoming desperate.

No other existing political system, or political theory, even begins to offer the absolute democratic safeguards which *All Party Alliance* can demonstrably guarantee. No other system can put an end for all time to autocratic one-party rule in Britain, and make its blood-brother, dictatorship (whether of the Left *or* Right) completely impossible.

No other existing plan to end Britain's constantly-recurring and economically disastrous industrial conflict even attempts what *Alliance in Industry* can achieve: *justice for both the Socialist who believes in nationalisation and the Conservative who believes in private enterprise.*

I believe that the change to *All Party Alliance*, in both its forms, is a natural, evolutionary step in the establishment *in fact* of the democratic rights which in theory are already ours. I have no doubt at all that when the principles and proposals of *All Party Alliance* government are fully known and understood the British people will not rest until the new system has become the law of the land.

At the moment, however, far too few know the facts, and while this book will give everyone at least a chance to learn, the need for these reforms is so obvious and so urgent that some more immediately effective method of telling the people is essential. I am quite sure that any one of our national newpapers which fully explained the principles of *All Party Alliance* to its readers today, would be astounded by the avalanche of approval evoked. Any national newspaper actively supporting the proposals could bring the system into being with dramatic suddenness.

Will any newspaper take up the challenge? Or any party?

. . . . . . . . . . . .

> "It is people as *citizens*, not as specialists, humanists, or scientists, who are going to decide the fate of the world."

H.R.H. The Prince Philip,
Duke of Edinburgh

# BOOK I

## ALL PARTY ALLIANCE

### Evolution to Political Democracy

# 2

It is a matter of simple fact that no society can truly prosper without the co-operation of its individual members. Only if a nation does prosper can all its people prosper.

Since a political system satisfying to at least the vast majority is an obvious pre-requisite of such co-operation, it follows that a properly-functioning democracy must provide the most fertile soil for a sound and flourishing economy. And since our present economic situation leaves so much to be desired, our political system must plainly be at fault. Under our existing system, moreover, there is considerable dissatisfaction at all social and income levels, and resentment, distrust and cynicism are increasingly widespread.

With interests represented by different parties and factions continually pulling against one another, industry and commerce consistently suffer major disruptions, often arising from the pettiest of disputes. Compared with our competitor nations, the growth of British productivity is slow and the quality of many of our products relatively poor. Service from supplier to consumer is too often negligent, inefficient, off-hand and unreliable, and this is true between retailer and customer at home and exporter and buyer abroad. For these reasons, we are simply not competitive in far too many fields. As a result, the gap between import and export is always too great, and we are in a state of constant crisis or near-crisis in our balance of payments with other nations.

At home, too, we shift from crisis to crisis, and are in continual danger from inflation. Almost without relief, the political and economic mood has for years been one of pessimism and gloom, punctuated by an occasional burst of unjustifiable optimism. Interests and mortage rates are penally high; taxation is held at a crippling level and in itself restricts industrial development—already slowed to a crawl by government restraints on bank-lending. Worst of all, and solely due to our industrial weaknesses, Great Britain—which fathered modern international banking and, with the Industrial Revolution, changed the whole course of world affairs to lead directly to this age of scientific achievement—is today a nation heavily in debt.

The effects of our unstable economic and political positions are as grave as they are obvious.

Commonwealth member nations have to seek financial and economic aid and even, on occasion, political guidance from non-member nations, including Russia. The countries of the Common Market so lacked confidence in us that for years none dared go against the dictates of a France revealed, in the event, to be in little better condition than ourselves. What influence we do exert in the world today is out of the seriously-depleting reserves of our past greatness, for international respect has to be underwritten by economic strength today just as much as in the past.

In the financial capitals of the world, a strong Britain is still deemed an essential cornerstone of Western security and economic growth. For that reason the World Bank, International Monetary Fund and 'lending' nations have consistently bolstered our economy by loans originally made to help us recover from the war and put our industrial and so our economic house in order. But a number of factors are clearly beginning to alarm world monetary sources:

1. The increasing indications that successive British Governments are coming to regard massive loans as automatic—to *expect* continuing help, whatever the circumstances.

2. The fact that much of our borrowing is simply to pay back earlier loans (or interest due on them).

3. The lack of any indication of successful attempts to deal with the problem at source: i.e. to increase our productivity and the quality of our goods—so 'working' instead of 'borrowing' our passage.

4. The growing conviction among some international bankers and political interests that we shall *never* be able to put our house in order, and so it is useless to continue to lend us money or extend us credit.

5. The fact that if this view should harden, and loans be refused or withdrawn, the pound would collapse, resulting not only in disaster for Great Britain and near-disaster for any Commonwealth country whose economy is integrated with our own, while also having serious repercussions on every Western currency and economy.

Plainly, the threat of this last eventuality, with its obvious advantages and opportunities for the Communist half of the world, is the basic reason for the continued support we at present receive from Western nations. It is equally plain that this help will one day be drastically curtailed if not actually withdrawn, simply because it can no longer be afforded, either materially or politically. There are limits to the economic resources of those nations on whom international funds depend; moreover, certain commercial interests in some powerful nations do not share the desire for an early revival of British economic strength.

These facts apart, it is unarguably in the vital interest not only of ourselves but of the whole free world, that Britain should begin forthwith to remove the causes and so the danger of economic collapse. For this, we must:

1. Bring our balance of payments into credit.

2. Keep our balance of payments in credit by economic growth, so that we become again a 'lending', not a 'borrowing' nation.

In plain language, Britain's first responsibility is to herself. Only by restoring her own fortunes can she pay her debts and meet her responsibilities to the world, and only when she has done so can she achieve the greatness which her history, her tradition, her wealth of experience and the qualities of her people deserve.

In the final analysis, after all, a nation's wealth lies in the qualities of its people, and the second World War alone proved just how great those qualities can be. Then, the people of Britain saw their responsibilities to the nation and the world, and shouldered them unhesitatingly: for those who needed guidance, Winston Churchill was the beacon lighting the way.

Duty in war is easier to define, however, and the goal is

obvious. The responsibilities of peacetime living are less apparent. Lack of urgency or recognisable common aim, ignorance of the essential interdependence of all individuals in any society, uninformed acceptance of prosperity at home at the expense of export trade and balance of payments—all these contributed to the deadly couldn't-care-less attitude so rife today.

The fault does not lie with those who cannot see, but with those who have failed to provide the beacon. To draw again on Britain's dormant seeds of greatness, we must first provide the unifying sense of mutual purpose and demonstrably mutual benefit which the war years evoked—and which indeed are essential before we can become a true democracy.

Great Britain is *allegedly* a representative democracy today, of course; but consider these facts:

1. For over thirty years, *no* party has gained office on a majority vote of the electors. Government has been by whichever party won most seats in the House of Commons at a General Election, even though millions more people voted against it, than for it.

2. Thus, under our present system, we are regularly subjected to one-party rule by a government which—*against the expressed wish of the majority*—can and does enact legislation based on the views and interests only of the minority it represents. The Opposition can voice its protests: it is completely powerless to do more.

3. When a minority-elected government has a large majority in the House of Commons, it can and does force through any legislation it wishes, riding roughshod over even the

most justified complaints of ambiguity and dubious intent in the phrasing of its Bills and flouting without compunction time-honoured parliamentary safeguards of consultation and advice.

4. When a minority-elected Government has a 'dangerously' small majority of elected Members, much time, energy and ingenuity are expended in peace-keeping between its own separate factions and otherwise maintaining the Government (party) position—leaving far too little for single-minded concentration on the affairs of the nation.

5. At the whim of any government, the country may be faced at any time with a General Election. The retiring Prime Minister may claim that the time has been chosen in the best interests of the nation: in fact, it is invariably chosen in the best interests of his party.

6. Finally, and perhaps most important of all, the present system makes it virtually impossible to have the nation's best political brains in the government. The most we can hope for is that the top posts will go to the best brains of the party in power. So inevitably, the services, special talents, and often invaluable experience of some exceptionally able men are constantly lost to the nation in sterile Opposition, while others, often far less able, carry the responsibility of ministerial duties.

These factors are at the root of all of Britain's troubles, simply because they fail in the first essential of true democracy: to give political justice to all men at all times. The evolution of our democracy, in the centuries since the

Levellers first stated the case for one man, one vote—"The poorest he that is in England hath a life to live, as the greatest he"—has been allowed to proceed along the wrong paths. It has given only an illusion of justice: an illusion naturally heightened by comparison with such liberty-denying doctrines as Fascism and Communism, both equally repugnant to a nation schooled since Magna Carta in the creed of personal and political freedom.

But true representative democracy is our birthright, and true representative democracy we must have.

What, then, *is* true democracy? There is no better definition than that supplied by Theodore Parker in a speech against slavery in 1850 and later enshrined for posterity by Abraham Lincoln at Gettysburg: "Government of the people, by the people, for the people." Which, in operative form, can only mean: "Government of *all* the people, by elected representatives of *all* the people—regardless of party—in the interests of *all* the people, *all* the time."

This is precisely what *All Party Alliance* can and will provide.

# 3

Here are the basic proposals for *All Party Alliance*:

1. A fixed term for each Parliament (say, four years) with a clearly-specified day for all General Elections; thus allowing the fullest opportunities for stable government.

2. General Elections to be fought (as now) on party lines, with each party working to win the largest share of the popular vote for its own policies—but with candidates and electors assured that *every vote will count, in the actual composition of the new Government.*

3. The leader of the party with most votes in the country to become Prime Minister.

4. The Prime Minister to appoint (a) his Cabinet and (b) his junior ministers from *all* the parties, in direct proportion to each party's share of the total vote.

5. Bills for debate to be drawn from each of the parties, in those same proportions.

6. No Bill before the House to be abandoned on grounds of

time: unfinished parliamentary business to be carried over to the next session.

7. The Party Whip system to be abolished and *every Bill submitted to a free vote of the House*.

The existence of different political parties is obviously essential to democracy. Each party simply comprises a group of people who share roughly the same beliefs, ideals and objectives: even if all Members of Parliament were independent, factions or parties of like-minded men would inevitably form. To abolish parties would be to abolish democracy.

But the 'two-party' system we have today does in all but name make democracy impossible, because all it really gives us is *absolute rule by one party, at all times*. Since 'the System' thus renders the attainment of power the prime political object, each party uses the constitution unashamedly to secure its own supremacy and so supreme control.

Under the present system, then, it is virtually impossible for the parties to work together. By the very nature of their imposed relationship, they *must* oppose each other—and thus, unavoidably, the interests of those who vote against them. Yet it would be a simple step to adapt the system so that the parties, instead of working against one another, were under compulsion to work together. Such a change would necessitate only one very minor change in accepted parliamentary convention.

It is perhaps not generally understood how much of parliamentary procedure is based on convention alone; through the years, these conventions have come to be so completely 'accepted' that all too often they are regarded as inviolable constitutional rules. There is, however, nothing in our laws to prevent the replacing of any existing convention by another. No constitutional change of any kind is required to establish government by *All Party Alliance*.

For example: the Constitution does not demand that a Member of Parliament should vote, in the House of Commons, as his party dictates. The *parties* (by convention) do. *All Party Alliance* would have him vote according to his conscience. The Constitution does not require him to accept the convention of discipline and command by Party Whip. The *parties* do.

The constitution indeed, demands that whether he fights for election as an Independent or as a party candidate, once in the House of Commons, he must represent not merely those who voted for him, but every elector in his constituency. Yet how can he hope to do so, with even elementary justice, if he must vote on every issue as his party dictates?

Convention alone decrees that, after a General Election, the leader of the party with the most Members in the House should automatically become Prime Minister. *There is no constitutional reason why the Sovereign should not instead invite the leader of the party with most votes in the country to form the new Government.* In this way, political justice would demonstrably be done: the voice of the people would be seen to be heeded; the will of the majority respected.

Moreover, the constitution does not demand that the Prime Minister fill all Cabinet and junior ministerial posts from his own party. There is ample peace- as well as wartime precedent for picking the best possible man for the job—choosing from all the parties, and from Independents. Under the present system, however, the parties themselves find promise or hope of office a powerful aid to discipline, and cynically ignore the obvious truth that no one party can have all the best brains, expertise and experience.

It is almost incredible how we have permitted our political system to come to this: government by one party, almost invariably minority-elected, which can and does impose its partisan policies on a whole nation.

That is not democracy. It is not even simple justice. Yet full justice to every man, woman and child in the nation can be ensured by moving from the present stage in the evolution of democracy to the next. It is not a long step, and it is an easy one. No harm can possibly come of it, and, once it is taken, for the first time in history a nation will be governed not only by a truly representative government, but by the very best men available, working together for the good of *all* the people.

Simple coalition is not the answer. It is simply government by one group of parties, with an Opposition made up of another group of parties. For the period of the government involved, both Government and Opposition are virtually single parties. Thus, coalition is much closer to single party government than it appears to be. However, coalition has one integral weakness greater than any in single party government. Any one of the parties joined together to form the coalition may withdraw at will, thus bringing the government down. It is this, particularly evident in France between the wars, which has brought coalitions into such disrepute. *All Party Alliance*, however, is coalition plus the strong democratic safeguards which are our right but which are today denied us. *All Party Alliance completely overcomes the weaknesses of simple coalition, while strengthening its obvious advantages.* *

To repeat: there is no constitutional reason why the Prime Minister should not choose his government from the best men of all the parties and from independents. It would be

*See Chapter 3.

unarguably just if he were to appoint (a) his Cabinet and (b) his junior ministers from each of the parties in direct proportion to the total vote cast for each party at the General Election. In this way, every elector would have, and know himself to have, direct representation *in the Government* at all times: not merely when 'his' party happened to be in power.*

The constitution, moreover, does not demand that all (save a few Private Members') Bills submitted to Parliament in any session should come from the same party: it simply requires that the Bills be submitted by Members of the House of Commons. Under the present system, the parties arrogate to themselves this 'right', when in power—that is: when nothing can prevent the passage of their Bills.

Thus, in thirteen years of Conservative Government, from 1951 to 1964, not a single Labour or Liberal Bill was submitted—nor, from 1945 to 1951, and 1964 to 1969, a single Conservative or Liberal Bill. Indeed, despite the millions of Liberal voters in Britain, no Liberal Bill has been debated—and no Liberal voter has had a 'voice' in government (except in coalition)—*for fifty years!*

Obviously it would be infinitely more just if the Bills debated in each Parliamentary session came from all the parties, in direct proportion to the votes cast for each at the General Election. Every elector who voted for a party out of respect for its policies would thus have a reasonable certainty of seeing Bills he believed good being given a fair chance of acceptance, in every session.

Can there be the slightest doubt that these simple evolutionary reforms would give the elector—and the M.P.—a

*The parties carefully foster the illusion that in Britain, every elector has a voice in his own government today. The fact is, the very great majority of voters are represented only in the debating-chamber: NOT in the Government itself.

much more direct say in the government of the nation?

*Can there be any doubt of their simple justice?*

We have forgotten, as a people, that democracy and justice to *all* the people are inseparable.

The examples of injustice in our present system are so glaring it is almost unbelievable that we allow them to continue.

For instance, there is neither constitutional nor just reason why the duration of every Parliament should be the uncertain—and economically damaging—gamble that it is today. It is the parties who maintain the system under which a General Election can be called at the will of the Prime Minister. Invariably he selects a moment he deems favourable to his party, no matter what injustice this may inflict on everyone else.

This is not elementary justice, yet we have accepted this convention for over a century.

There is no Constitutional reason why the time accorded to Private Members' Bills should be so disturbingly inadequate. As things are today, parliamentary time would be too short to allow the equitable division of Bills even among the parties. But there is no Constitutional reason why each Parliament should not endure for a fixed term of four years, say, so that the date of the next General Election is always known. Thus all parties, all electoral offices—and all would-be candidates, incidentally,—would be given an equal chance to prepare for it. And there is no constitutional reason why the business of one session should not automatically be carried over to the next, so that no Bill, by whomsoever sponsored, could ever again be thrown out simply for want of parliamentary time.

As, under *All Party Alliance*, every party would have a share in government and a share in Bills presented, there would always be time for a proper debate.* The Party Whip system would be abolished so as to give each Bill a fair chance (and so each elector a fair deal). The Party Whip, after all, is a creation of the parties themselves, and, as its name implies, was conceived and is used to whip the party member into obedience. It serves no constitutional purpose of any kind whatsoever. It serves party interest against national interest. It frequently compels Members of Parliament to vote against their real beliefs: with very rare exceptions, the most a dissenting Member dare do is abstain from voting at all, where in honesty he could only vote in opposition. In other words, under the present system, a party Member can in effect be 'forced' to opt out of his obligations to his constituents, his country and his conscience.

With *All Party Alliance*, as we have seen, there would be a free vote of the House on every issue. With each Member voting according to his own judgement and conviction, a completely new and just situation would exist in the House of Commons. Each Bill would be debated on its merits. A Right-wing Labour M.P. or Left-wing Conservative could vote openly against the party-line on a particular Bill, without fear of losing his party's trust and so endangering his political future. On certain issues, obviously, one party or another would be strongly united: but its unity would be born of genuine belief, not fear of consequences.

Politicians more concerned with party supremacy and power than public interest, have tried to dismiss the proposals as 'unworkable' between opposed parties. But, just as the parties work brilliantly together in time of war, *because they have no choice,* they will make the new system work if enough electors demand that they do so. Once they have seen the

*See Chapter 4.

advantages to themselves, the majority of politicians will support the proposals of their own accord.

There are a number of perfectly valid questions, which could probably only be answered to the complete satisfaction of all by a Commission specifically established to examine the proposals. It is possible, however, to submit answers which in themselves are equally valid. Thus:

*How would the Prime Minister select his Ministers?*

Clearly, he would (as now) select those from his own party personally. For the posts to be filled from other parties, he should ask for nominations from each party (say, ten for every seven posts allotted it by the national vote) and make his choice from the names so submitted. These nominees should be the popular choice of their fellow party Members in the House.

*What would prevent the Prime Minister from giving all the 'plum' posts to members of his own party?*

As the Cabinet posts would have to be shared, these 'plums' would necessarily go to each party in direct proportion to the popular vote. Political journalists and commentators would ensure that the country at large knew the proportion of posts due to each. (Take, for example, the 1966 General Election figures: with *All Party Alliance*, a Cabinet of twenty, today, would have nine Labour, eight Conservative, and three Liberal and/or Independent Members; and the proportions for junior ministerial posts would be: forty-five Labour, forty Conservative, fifteen Liberal and others.)

# THE BASIC PROPOSALS

*Often with as few as ten or eleven Members of Parliament, how could the Liberals fill their share?*

From the House of Lords, until such time as the number of the M.P.s more closely represented the Liberal vote in the country—which it predictably would, after a General Election which guaranteed to Liberal voters that their every vote would count. Only then will the true Liberal strength in the country be known.

*How could Conservatives and Liberals possibly come to terms with Socialists on such issues as, for instance, nationalisation?*

Part two of this book explains a system under which all parties, and Independents, could come to mutually acceptable terms, without loss of honour to any.

*The fundamental purpose of All Party Alliance is to create government by ALL the parties—in direct ratio to the public will—and thus, it follows, based on the POLICIES of all the parties.*

Obviously, it will demand compromise; but here I believe the British instinct for fair play will prove to be the nation's greatest asset. No honest man who values his own right to speak and vote and strive for his personal ideal society will deny another man an equal right. When men agree to differ in the cause of human progress, there can only be honour in mutual concession.

An electorate convinced that *All Party Alliance* was the right system of government would simply instruct the parties to get together and work out the best and most practicable policy for the nation. In other words, a democratic people would at last be able to ensure that it was led by a democratic government. The final word would always be with the people, the electorate, in a system which would be safe against the political chicanery so brazenly, and almost inevitably, rife today.

No vote could ever again be wasted: every vote would truly count. The present public disenchantment with politics and politicians would dissolve dramatically as the people recognised that all their views and all their wishes would at all times be effectively represented in the government itself—and so in the nation's policies and legislation.

Clearly, each party would operate at its best, since each could concentrate on formulating policy and preparing convincing arguments in its support. Because each would know that no Bill would ever again be 'automatically' bulldozed through Parliament, or 'automatically' opposed on party grounds—that every Bill which was patently in the public interest would stand an excellent chance of passage into law.

Clearly, too, the leaders and other exceptionally able members of each party would always be in office, their expertise and experience available at all times instead of, as now, being lost to the nation's service in powerless 'Opposition' and futile Shadow Cabinet for years at a time.

Ministerial appointment could thus be based on experience and ability; not, as so often today, on expediency. Ministerial changes, moreover, would at last be dictated by national, not by party interest. In the sensitive field of international relations, the fact that key posts could be filled, irrespective of party, would be a tremendous advantage. Since basic national policies would be thrashed out between *all* the parties, other nations would be able to rely on continuity of basic British policy in all Commonwealth and foreign affairs.

Nor would the change of system affect the normal conduct of Cabinet affairs. Under the present system, the Prime Minister is simply 'the first among equals': expected to act as chairman, with the power of decision and of reconciling conflicting views—as, whatever his party, he is constantly required to do today. Why should he experience any more difficulty in presiding over an all-party Cabinet of highly-intelligent men who all know they must reach reasonable compromise, and among whom his own supporters predominate?

*Could any Prime Minister truly concerned with the nation's best interests ask anything better than the chance to choose his Cabinet from all the nation's best political brains?*

Obviously, these political changes would not in themselves adjust the national economy. But they could hardly fail to improve the temper and spirit of the people, and so create, at long last, the climate of national opinion essential for a successful drive to win back economic prosperity.

Later chapters of this book deal specifically with the industrial and commercial aspects of the nation's existence. Before discussing them, however, the political aspects need further amplification.

# 4

We have examined the reasons for the decline of the present system: how the nation is governed not by true representation of the people, but—in turn—by the major parties, each virtually driven *by* the system to put the achievement of power and control before the championing of democratic rights or the public will.

We have seen how the new system of *All Party Alliance* would remove the cause of all the utterly futile hostility between the parties and compel all to work together in the national interest. We have also seen that, far from raising any constitutional issue, the proposed changes would actually give us, in fact, the government (and the political justice) which our constitution is already supposed to guarantee us all.

It is my belief that the solutions to all the problems of present-day democracies are inherent in *All Party Alliance*. It is a fact that in four by-elections, campaigners from all parties exerted themselves to deride and discredit the A.P.A. proposals, but none succeeded.

There was a persistent attempt to obscure the real meaning of the proposals; and *every* party openly strove—either with cynical unconcern for truth, or with singularly ironic naïveté—to depict *All Party Alliance* as a threat to democracy. There would be no Opposition, they cried. It would just be one great, conglomerate one-party dictatorship! And with some voters, inevitably, they managed to make these calumnies 'stick'.

The parties worked, of course, on the principle that the more people could be frightened by talk of a threat to the imagined status quo, the less chance there would be of their recognising the truth: that our existing system is a travesty of democracy. That it is this very system, this spurious democracy, which subjects us to one-party dictatorship; to absolute, one-party rule at all times, whichever the party in power. That it is this present system which denies us—and has denied us for over a century—the democratic protection of an effective Opposition.

*All Party Alliance,* on the other hand, is the only political system which can absolutely guarantee to make one-party rule—and its blood-brother, dictatorship—completely imposs-ible. A free vote of the House, on EVERY Bill, is the strongest democratic safeguard we could possibly have.

This is because the Opposition, as well as the government, would be made up of M.P.s from all the parties. The Opposition's purpose would not, as now, be automatically to oppose every issue on party lines: to harrass, embarrass and discredit the government of the day in the hope of defeating it at a General Election. Instead, reasoned argument would develop against each Bill as it was presented, in the same way as support would develop—based on honest judgement of the Bill's merits. Obviously a Conservative Bill would get its main support from members of that party. But Labour or Liberal M.P.s could, without danger to themselves or damage to their parties, vote for it if they believed it to be in the nation's interest. In exactly the same way, Conservatives who could not in honesty support it would be perfectly free to vote against it.

## THE BENEFITS INHERENT IN A.P.A.

Thus *All Party Alliance* would remove one of the most difficult and invidious of parliamentary dilemmas: the all too often enforced choice between party loyalty and personal conscience—between official approval and disfavour.

The present sprinkling of Liberals and others, of course, can already vote without danger to themselves—but equally without effect to the issue. Even today's handful of Liberals have their Whips. If they—and similarly the Scottish and Welsh Nationalist M.P.s—are to retain their personal integrity, along with their party's support, their present freedom of conscience must be established as an unchallengeable right, before their parliamentary numbers increase.

*How, without a free vote of the House, can there ever BE honesty, or justice, in Parliament?*

Without a free vote, how can we hope that any legislation will truly be in the best interests, and faithfully reflect the democratic will of *all* the nation?

Can anyone doubt that, had the latest Steel Nationalisation Bill been submitted to a free vote of the House a number of Right-wing Socialists would have voted against it? Or that the various 'Squeeze' measures of the 1960s, culminating in the Wages and Incomes Policy, would—given a free vote—have had a much rougher passage? Labour M.P.s *had* to vote as the Party Whips dictated, or 'betray' their party: only the exceptionally courageous even abstained.

*Any parliamentary system which regularly demands such cynical sacrifice of private conscience to party interest must, by its very nature, destroy itself.*

*Conversely, a system which not only makes such situations impossible, but enables all M.P.s to vote freely and honestly according to the merits of each Bill, MUST, by its very nature, nurture and strengthen parliamentary democracy.*

# EVOLUTION TO DEMOCRACY

But how, the sceptics will ask, can there be strong and stable government when even now each party is frequently divided within itself on various issues?

The answer is simple: with a fixed four-year term, the government as such could never be brought down, either by opposition or by internal revolt. *Only the Bill before the House could be defeated.* If the Bill carried with it a vote of confidence in the sponsoring Minister, its defeat could and should mean his resignation; but he would be replaced from within his own party. *No Prime or other Minister could continue to hold office against the wish of the majority of Members.*

The crucial factor is that opposition would be to each Bill; it would never be to the government as such. Extremists from each party would predictably vote against one another on idealogical issues, but on certain non-idealogical issues (e.g. Road Safety, Capital Punishment, the Divorce Laws and Public Health) even these extremists might well vote together—as indeed some already do, on the rare occasions when the Government permits a free vote.

(A memorable illustration of how this free-forming support and opposition would work occurred in 1958, when a free vote was allowed on an issue of parliamentary privilege. The then Mr. Herbert Morrison, Labour M.P., led most of the Conservatives into the 'No' Lobby, while the then Mr. R.A. Butler, Lord Privy Seal and Leader of the House, led most of the Labour M.P.s into the 'Aye'.)

The inherent evil in the present system is that a free vote (on the grounds of conscience) is permitted only at the will of the government. That is, at the will of the party in power, which often means the will of two or three members of the Cabinet—and far too often, the will of the Prime Minister alone. *The inherent GOOD in All Party Alliance is that no M.P. would EVER need special permission to do what he believed to be right.*

The granting to every M.P. of what is already his constitutional right, to be accountable only to his conscience and his constituents, simultaneously with the sweeping away of ethically indefensible pressures, imposed in the name of party loyalty, would bring such an upsurge of self-respect and enthusiasm as to virtually transform the parliamentary scene.

Instead of a resentfully-submissive 'rubber-stamp' government party and a resentfully frustrated 'rubber-stamp' Opposition, every M.P. would assume his true importance in the nation's life as the elected champion of tens of thousands of tax-paying citizens, and co-protector of the democratic rights of all the rest. There would also be a completely new spirit and pace in the conduct of the nation's business. No party would even wish to waste precious parliamentary time in petty bickering and political point-scoring or indulging in opposition for opposition's sake, at a time when delay of any business must inevitably lead to delay in presentation of its own next Bill.

This new sense of honesty and justice in politics would of itself create a completely new spirit in the country. Voters everywhere would be alert to see which party sponsored most Bills in the true national interest; and when it came to an election, would give that party more votes, more members in the Government, more Bills to sponsor. If any party demonstrably failed to sponsor Bills for the national good, the electors could and assuredly would reduce its representation in the next government. Yet neither the party so patently out of favour, nor any other of the minority parties (and so voters) would ever be denied the right to a proportionately effective voice in the nation's affairs.

Now let us see how the proposals would affect the individual aspects of our parliamentary system.

## THE EFFECT ON THE PRIME MINISTER

The fact that the leader of a one-party government with an impotent Opposition has—and uses—the power to dispense favours for past services, to strengthen his own position by open manipulation of sudden peerage and 'safe seat', to pacify by bribe or inducement rebellious party members, is why there is so much cynicism in and so much disgust with politics today: such widespread acceptance that politics is a dirty business.

How can it possibly be otherwise under a system which positively encourages abuse and misuse of political power?

With *All Party Alliance,* a party leader having favours to dispense, would never dare to misuse his influence. He would be too conscious of the watchful eyes of all the Members of all the parties. He would have to play fair, or risk being overwhelmingly defeated, disgraced and displaced.

Nor need there ever be any fear of secret pacts among the parties. For news of such a pact would leak out, and some member would object. No longer in danger of becoming a political exile by being honest, he would speak up to a House able at long last to be jealous of its own integrity.

Yet another ill-founded objection to A.P.A. by politicians loath to relinquish their own party's present or prospective enjoyment of absolute power is that, with all the parties represented in the government, we should in effect have government by committee.

The truth is that government by committee, in the

derogatory sense, is seen at its most iniquitous in the present system of *Orders in Council,* by which a sub-committee of the Cabinet can virtually demand the Queen's assent to a law *before* it is debated in the House. The Committee Stage, where a Bill comes in for detailed examination by 'a Committee reflecting party representation in the House', has all the trappings of democracy, but—since the passage of every Government Bill is a foregone conclusion*—none of the substance.

## THE CABINET

The Cabinet itself, of course, is nothing more or less than a Committee of senior ministers. Under the present system, it makes its decisions without consulting other parties—indeed, it does not consult its own. It then gives the Minister concerned virtual dictatorial authority to implement the committee decision. The Minister may bring pressure to bear on employers and Trade Unions alike to 'persuade' them to comply, and he has powers to compel 'co-operation' if they do not.

This is government by committee at its worst.

With *All Party Alliance,* every Bill would depend for its passage upon the majority approval of a freely-voting House, so even majority-party members of a committee would have a very real incentive to find and eradicate any flaws in their own party's Bills. Committee members opposed to a Bill would be equally alert for and ready to fight inherent injustices or weaknesses not 'cured' at the Committee Stage.

*The two government back-bench M.P.s who dared, earlier this year, to raise valid objections to important proposals in the new Children and Young Persons Bill, claim they were swiftly removed from its Committee by pressure from ministerial level.

# EVOLUTION TO DEMOCRACY

Instead of one-party Cabinet dictatorship, a Minister would have to win majority support from his all-party colleagues before any single piece of legislation was approved, before any Order in Council received royal assent.

*This is not 'government by committee': it is government by a parliament which truly represents ALL the electors.*

Nor would this mean the slightest slowing-down of decision-making or Cabinet business generally. In wartime, decisions affecting the lives of millions were an everyday occurrence. Yet Winston Churchill could still demand: "ACTION THIS DAY!" *and get it*—with a coalition government!

Obviously, under the new system, the calibre of the Cabinet would be greatly improved, and national and international respect for Britain's leadership increased. Since each party would need to find fewer candidates for high office than in a one-party administration, and since each party would have the right to be and would obviously wish to be represented in the government to best possible advantage, these nominees would predictably be the ablest and most experienced the parties could muster.

Selection for government office would of course remain the prerogative of the Prime Minister, whose sole obligation would be to ensure that the appointments were made in the stipulated proportion of the national vote and in the national interest. But with the best men of each party to choose from, the task of finding ministers of the desired exceptional ability and qualifications would be much less difficult than it often is today. Since some nominees would be obvious choices for specific posts, the formation of a new government would be much more simply and speedily accomplished.

Moreover, with *All Party Alliance*, a notably successful

Minister could win deserved re-appointment or new office after a General Election *whether or not* the leader of his party became Prime Minister. Thus, the rewards for maximum efficiency and dedication to the national interest—and even more essential, the *incentives* without which we cannot hope to attract the nation's best men into politics—will at last have been provided.

*ALL PARTY ALLIANCE*, IN SHORT, IS THE ONLY POLITICAL SYSTEM WHICH CAN ENSURE THAT THE PEOPLE'S CHOSEN REPRESENTATIVES WILL BE COMPELLED TO SERVE THE NATION WITH ABSOLUTE INTEGRITY, THE HIGHEST POSSIBLE EFFICIENCY, AND JUSTICE TO US ALL.

## LEADERSHIP

One of the most noticeable and surely most significant features of the modern British political scene is the absence of outstanding men. There has been no truly great leader since Sir Winston Churchill. No one has caught and held the public imagination in the way of Disraeli, Gladstone, Balfour, Lloyd George, Ramsay MacDonald, Sir Stafford Cripps, Philip Snowden, Baldwin and even Bonar Law.

The existing political system makes it increasingly difficult for the brilliant individualist, the potential statesman, the 'born leader', to find scope for his talents, his energy and his radical new ideas, where they are most needed: in the government and guidance of the nation. Directly a man of promise joins a party, he has to conform to the party line and—the greatest barrier, to men of integrity—be prepared either to put party dictate before what he may deem wiser counsel, or sink into political oblivion.

# EVOLUTION TO DEMOCRACY

Industry, commerce, banking, the sciences and the arts can all boast men of outstanding ability and even genius, who would willingly—and at great personal sacrifice—put their talents and specialised knowledge at the country's service. Today, even when such men *are* brought into the government, their work may all too likely be negatived in the interests of political expediency.

Under the present system, an exceptionally able man can agree to serve the nation, only to find that the government which asked him to do so has changed its standpoint on a major policy issue—or else has abruptly become the Opposition. In either case, although he may barely have begun a project needing years to bring to fruition, he is 'out'.

We *must* have men of real stature at the nation's helm, and, assuredly, they do exist. However, we cannot expect men to leave the work they do superlatively well, with its commensurately high rewards in both money and prestige, for a task they will almost certainly never be allowed to finish.

Nor can we blame the young men of great promise who reject the political arena for fields where integrity has real value, and ability real scope. Indeed, under the present system, there is virtually nothing to attract into government men of calibre, experience and breadth of vision the country so desperately needs.

With *All Party Alliance,* any outstanding business or professional figure, invited by the government to take a post of national importance, could accept in the knowledge that the job would be his for as long as he did it well. Since the invitation would have prior approval from an all-party majority, he would not be 'thrown out' by a change of heart in either party or electorate. Moreover, the very knowledge that support for his selection came from 'all sides' would give him every incentive to make a brilliant success of the post.

Similarly, there would be real scope and incentive for the career-politician. If he distinguished himself in debate or in office, he would be almost certain to find his special qualities utilised not only by his own party, but by any party leader facing the task of forming a government.

## MEMBERS OF PARLIAMENT

Under the present system, as we have seen, a party M.P. is virtually compelled to represent only those who voted for him, even if—as often happens—more of his constituents have voted against him than for him. Many M.P.s try to compensate for this by taking a deep interest in the local conditions affecting their constituents of all parties. This does not alter the fact that M.P.s today are effectively forced to ignore even the most valid arguments in favour of policies supported by those who voted against them.

With *All Party Alliance,* the abolishment of the Party Whip means that M.P.s could safely vote as conscience dictated, even on the most controversial issues.

Thus, on matters affecting the particular social, economic and industrial well-being of their constituencies, they would be able at last to vote without guilt in what they believed the best interests of all their constituents. Moreover, with the electors aware that *all* their views were represented and all the policies they supported would have champions at all times in the government itself, an M.P. would earn nothing from his local electorate but respect for his honesty.

The establishment of public trust in parliamentary integrity would be a source of enormous moral strength to all M.P.s, as well as a powerful incentive to give of their absolute best. The ending of the 'automatic' political exile which today occurs whenever their party fails to win most of the seats at a General Election, would be another great spur to endeavour. With a fixed four-year term for each Parliament, every M.P., standing a good chance of winning office under any party leader, would exert himself to be scrupulously fair in every respect.

For those already in the Cabinet or in junior ministries, the four-year term would give much greater scope for really imaginative long-term plans, so providing even greater opportunity for conspicuous personal success.

Above all, *every* M.P. would have the very great satisfaction of knowing that his voice, and his vote—whether for *or* against any piece of legislation—would always be of positive importance.

## THE PARTIES

Under the present system, the need to project an outwardly unified 'party image' in the hope of winning elections, or for other reasons pretend 'solidarity' and 'strength', is in fact a party's greatest weakness.

It has to become all things to all men: has to trim its sails, and so its principles simply with a view to winning over wavering or uncommitted voters. Its leaders will hedge or actually change ground, on major and on minor issues. Its true policies and purposes become obscured: its 'image' increasingly faceless.

At conferences and in committee, too, each party caucus constantly tries to soothe or silence rebellious elements; constantly seeks a formula which will both satisfy its members and attract more votes.

This continual polishing of the party image in the public

eye has a debilitating effect on the party itself. Members to the right or left of the official (vote-catching) line, brought to heel by threat or disciplinary action, invariably continue to seethe with discontent, being afraid to speak their true minds for fear of harming party election prospects.

Yet it is very often the aggressively forward-thinking rebels who give a party not only its most imaginative new ideas, but the fresh vigour and vitality best calculated to win the uncommitted and the younger vote. *All Party Alliance* would give all such rebels ample scope, without driving them to frustration and open revolt as does the present system. It would also give the rebels, in fact all true progressives in all parties, ample room to develop their own qualities. Men of great ability would have a much better chance of reaching the top of their party, and so men of the highest calibre would always be available for government office.

At present, the majority (government) party has about one hundred ministerial posts to fill. Many, as we have seen, must go to men who are inexperienced, uninspired, and all too often depressingly inept.

With *All Party Alliance,* even on the 1966 poll, the majority party would have to fill only fifty-odd posts. Since proven ability or valuable experience would be a basic requirement for office, the resultant competition would be like a shot in the arm to each party. For, clearly, the man who kept his post with support from all the parties would command much more respect, both at home and abroad, than one whose party will support him, right or wrong.

If a series of by-elections changed the balance of power in the House, the Prime Minister could be defeated on a vote of confidence and replaced by the leader of the new majority party*—but the government would not fall.

*i.e. The party with the most *votes* in the country, *not* seats in the House.

Thus, with *All Party Alliance*, each party would have constant incentive to improve the calibre of its leadership, and so of its parliamentary candidates. Moreover, with each party able to sponsor Bills in every session of Parliament, the necessity of winning support would ensure a constant reviewing of existing policies and a lively concern to find imaginative solutions to problems arising from prevailing conditions or current events. There would be no sense or advantage in 'watering-down' party policy to make it more 'acceptable'.

*The only way to win majority all-party approval would be to ensure that the Bill submitted is palpably WORTHY of support and the case for it presented with complete lucidity.*

## IMPROVED LEGISLATION

Under the present system, as we have seen, nearly every Bill presented to the House of Commons is sponsored by one political party (the government) and based on that party's policy. Even when a Bill seems clearly against the national interest or clearly against the people's will, the Opposition today is completely powerless to prevent its passage. Nor has it even the power to insist that Bills presented are clearly comprehensible!

In consequence, the Bills ostensibly submitted for the consideration and approval of the whole House are frequently ill-prepared and unintelligibly or ambiguously phrased. These almost automatically become law, however, no matter how vigorously the Opposition (or the government's own back-benchers) may protest. Experienced civil servants, accountants and other professional men often find the interpretation, and so the enforcement, of these laws extremely difficult.

Far too much valuable time and skill is wasted today simply through these unwarrantable defects in legislation.

With *All Party Alliance*, every successful Bill would have gained on its own merits the support of a majority of freely-voting M.P.s of *all* parties. The preparation of each Bill would thus of necessity be considerably more thorough, and its lucidity assured before presentation.

With the Bill itself thus made more readily comprehensible, and with all parties having equal opportunity to study its clauses and conditions well in advance, the standard of debates at the First (and later) Reading and Committee Stages would obviously be considerably higher than it is today. With every Member fully conversant with the Bill's basic proposals, and thus able to offer constructive criticism or valid objection, the views of all would be taken into account throughout.

Since each party would sponsor its own quota of Bills, it would obviously benefit none to obstruct, solely for the sake of obstruction, those sponsored by others. Only by taking a constructive attitude towards all Bills could any party be sure of the same fair-minded approach towards its own.

## BENEFITS TO THE ELECTORS

We come finally to the effect of *All Party Alliance* on the electors, as a whole and as individuals.

It is a simple fact that respect and desire for 'fair play' is ingrained in the British character. Yet, under our present political system, only once in forty years has a British government been elected by a true majority. Despite the party's huge majority in the House of Commons, *three out of five electors did not vote for a Labour Government in 1966.*

# EVOLUTION TO DEMOCRACY

Millions upon millions of votes, almost always more than half the total poll, are quite simply nullified and so utterly wasted, at every General Election. Millions upon millions more are not even used, as public disgust at the blatant injustice of 'the system', and resentment at the politicians who uphold it, becomes increasingly widespread.

*All Party Alliance* would eradicate both the cause, and the lamentable effects, of these injustices. It cannot be said too often that no vote would ever be wasted: every vote would be of real significance in deciding the actual composition of the government. Even if 'his' candidate failed to win, every elector would know that his *vote* would go to strengthen his party's voice in the nation's affairs.

As each party would sponsor important legislation during each session of parliament, even minority party supporters would know that the policies they believed in would have a fair chance of becoming law. And the independent-minded, who today rarely vote because, while they find acceptable policies in each party's 'platform', they cannot fully approve of any, would be able in all good conscience to vote, at last—"for the man, not for the party."

If a Bill the public deemed to be in the national interest were defeated in one Parliament, the voters could (as now) ensure its passage in the next, simply by ensuring a majority total vote for the sponsoring party's candidates at the next General Election.

With the assurance of political fair play for all inherent in *All Party Alliance*, the present public revulsion from politics and politicians would soon disappear. Until we actually create a climate of mutual respect and trust, however, we cannot hope to evoke the sense of common purpose, the national team spirit, so urgently needed to compete successfully with the rest of the world. In time of war coalition brings these qualities, but there are grave weaknesses in peace-time coalition: weaknesses which can lead to disaster.

*All Party Alliance* can eliminate those weaknesses; and in order to see how, we need to go over some ground already touched upon in earlier chapters.

# 5

No one can doubt that in time of war, a sense of common purpose forges the British people and parties into a team of unbeatable strength, always through coalition. War, quite demonstrably, brings out the best in all the people. They perform wonders; they win against impossible odds.

*United, they have proved themselves unbeatable.*

After victory, however, the politicians lose no time in shattering this magnificent team spirit. The peace which followed two world wars brought disaster upon disaster to Britain.

Instead of uniting in proven strength to overcome the common problems of the transition from war- to peace-time economy, the winning team splits into party factions which fight among themselves. In disunity, they throw away the fruits of a victory paid for—at incalculable cost in suffering and sacrifice—by those people whom they set out to govern.

So, the obvious question is: why not have government by coalition in peacetime? It seems the obvious answer, and opinion polls have shown that a high percentage of the people believe it could be the right one. However, most politicians appear to hate the very thought.

Why?

Many love power for power's sake, and revel in their share

of the dictatorial power inherent in one-party government. Far more, of course, simply stubbornly believe that no party's policies could be better than their own, and until they are actually required to do so, by the system, will refuse even to consider the merits of any others.

But a great many really do fear that conflicts of policy inside a coalition government could cause the kind of chaos exampled by the farcical French administrations of the pre- De Gaulle era, or else conditions which have so damaged the Labour and the Liberal parties in the past.

Without the ready co-operation obligatory at times of national emergency, simple coalition might indeed do this. To ensure really strong and stable government at all times, to safeguard the people's democratic rights, to engender the mutual trust and sense of common purpose with which to inspire all parties, all politicians, and all the people to give of their best in time of peace, coalition needs a 'plus'.

This plus is provided by *All Party Alliance*. We have already seen that *All Party Alliance* requires no constitutional changes, and can be brought about as quickly and easily as simple coalition. It could be in operation tomorrow, based on the figures for the last General Election. But its real significance lies in its fundamental differences from coalition:

A *coalition,* as we have known it, is an interim government formed by some or all (or sections of some of all) of the parties, to meet a national emergency.

*All Party Alliance* is a permanent system of government which demands and ensures the highest service of the nation's interests by all the parties, all the time.

# COALITION PLUS

*Coalition* is government by agreement between consenting parties or groups only, and may bear no slightest relation to the political preferences of the voting public.

*All Party Alliance* is government by all the parties in direct ratio to the will of the people, as demonstrated by the poll at each General Election.

A *coalition government* can be brought down by defeat by its opponents in the House. Such a government might last for only a few months.

With *All Party Alliance,* a government Bill may be defeated, but the government would not fall. Each government would serve for a term of four years, followed automatically by a General Election. If a Bill's defeat brought about a vote of no confidence in the Administration, the Prime or any other Minister would resign or be voted out of office by the House, and be replaced from within his own party.

In a peacetime *coalition,* fear of opposition which might bring down the government means that the only legislation possible is that which will offend no one.

With *All Party Alliance,* each party may introduce the most challenging of Bills with a fair chance of winning sufficient support from members of the other parties to make it law, or their constructive help in making it viable.

In certain circumstances, coalitions can be stronger than one-party governments: those formed in Britain to fight the First and Second World Wars were outstandingly successful during the crisis periods. But once peace was on the way, the parties began seeking their own political advantage in a bid for absolute power.

*That is the basic weakness of peacetime coalition. It is vulnerable to attack from within: either from the defection of a member party, which could bring down the government, or from domination by one party through threat of such defection.*

The whole structure of *All Party Alliance* ensures that all parties and all Members of Parliament must put the nation's interest first, without waiting for a crisis—and makes it unarguably to their advantage to do so. If they do not, they themselves will be the first to suffer.

No party could ever dominate an *All Party Alliance* government. By its very nature, it must always serve the interests of all the parties and all the people, all the time.

So, I repeat: with the powerful opposition which could be mustered in a free vote of the House, *All Party Alliance* is the ONLY form of government which can make dictatorship in any form completely impossible.

The weaknesses, and the palpable failure of successive peacetime coalitions in France led, almost inevitably, to one-party government under General de Gaulle. Just as inevitably, this government led to the rebellion which was so near revolution, in the spring of 1968. This path towards dictatorship is innate in all the present forms of parliamentary democracy. It was seen at its alarming and saddening worst in Greece—the birthplace of democracy—when, overnight, tanks and a military junta replaced the vote. The inherent faults within each system lead, sooner or later, to economic weakness, which in turn leads to 'firmer' control by the politicians in power.

This has been as evident in West Germany as in France, and the contemptuous ease with which successive British governments today ride roughshod over all opposition, shows how dangerously close we have come to acceptance of neo-dictatorial government here.

As recently as May, 1969, the Labour Government seriously considered the appointment of a ministerial overlord for the efficiency of all nationalised industries.

"This proposal for a *supremo* to boss all the State industries was recommended in a report by the Select Committee on National Industries last September. Under this plan, the Minister would have become, in practice, the Minister for Heavy Industry, with a Ministry under him supervising the running of all the state-owned boards."*

Let us examine this more closely.

The nationalised industries, while technically responsible to Parliament, are actually autonomous. But link them together, and a form of industrial dictatorship would come into existence automatically. Bring this vast complex under the direct control of the government—in the name of the state—and there would be virtual dictatorship.

Another dangerous threat to our democratic rights is inherent in the recurring calls for 'a businessmen's government' to meet crisis situations. The need to strengthen the government with men of outstanding ability and achievement in industry and commerce is very great. But a government exclusively of such men, created to meet a crisis—and thus

*Sunday Times, 25.5.69.

with a strong case for using emergency powers—might well lead to the crushing of all opposition.

In the short term, the material results might be good, as they were in France until the 1968 rebellion, but in the long term, such a form of government could only lead to revolt. The resultant hardening of antagonism between government and workers would simply lead to worsening productivity ratios, and bring the economy to an even more critical state.

The national need to produce enough goods at fully competitive prices, in a highly-competitive world, is very real and very urgent. But no government can hope to achieve a flourishing economy without the co-operation and support of the people. An imposed, increasingly dictatorial, unrepresentative government will not win that co-operation and support from a disenchanted and grossly-overtaxed electorate, the great majority of whom blame the plight of the nation on the policies and shortcomings of its leadership—and deeply resent being asked to foot the bill.

Nor, of course, is this disenchantment with the political scene confined to Britain. Indeed, I believe that it can only be a matter of time before all existing forms of parliamentary democracy begin to fail. The world needs a viable alternative to present forms of democracy: a system which will truly guarantee political and social justice to *all* the people *all* the time. In short, we need a powerful Opposition which no government, no party, no form of coalition, can possibly crush. For democracy can only flourish if the Opposition to the government is unfettered and can play an immediate and vital part in the nation's affairs.

If my conclusions are justified, then *All Party Alliance alone can provide such an Opposition*. No other existing political system can ensure the absolute safeguards to true 'representative democracy'. Re-stated in simplest terms, the principles of the new system ensure that:

THE PEOPLE would elect the PRIME MINISTER—the leader of whichever party won the MOST VOTES at each General Election.

CABINET MINISTERS would be drawn from EACH party, in direct proportion to the popular vote . . . All other government posts would be allocated in that same proportion.

*So, no vote is wasted: every vote counts—in the choice of Prime Minister, in the political composition of his Cabinet, and in the framing and passage of all future legislation.*

ALL M.P.s could vote freely on EVERY issue . . . No more WHIPS telling them what to do . . . No more threats or inducements to vote against conscience or common sense.

*So, M.P.s have nothing to lose by honesty—and everything to gain. Are enabled, at last, to truly represent ALL their constituents, as they are constitutionally intended to do.*

GENERAL ELECTIONS would be held on a SPECIFIED DAY, EVERY FOUR YEARS—*not* at the whim, or for the party advantage, of the government in power . . .

THE PRIME MINISTER or any other Minister would be forced to resign if the MAJORITY of M.P.s (representing

ALL the people) think he should . . . But the government would not fall: Ministers would be replaced from their own parties.

*So, we get stable government at all times, yet with no fear that a discredited or power-obsessed Prime Minister might remain in office against the public will.*

In essence, then, *All Party Alliance* means:

No more Party Whips . . . No risk of dictatorship . . . Conservatives, Socialists, Liberals, Scottish and Welsh Nationalists—all parties and Independents—always represented in the government yet always free to vote against it.

THE OPPOSITION would thus have bite, not merely bark. It would be able, at last, actually to prevent the waste or misuse of taxpayers' money, and to stop bad Bills from becoming law.

Members of Parliament of all parties, truly representing all the people, would have the right to oppose any Bill they believed against public interest, and to insist on clarification of ambiguously phrased, badly drafted Bills, before passage.

*So the Opposition would become, at long last, the effective watchdog of the nation's interests and the people's rights, which is its fundamental democratic role.*

In today's world, however, political, social and industrial issues are so interdependent and interwoven that there can be no justice in any if there is injustice in one. Democracy is as vital in industry and commerce as it is in politics. The present system of single-control and ownership of any industry, or any branch of industry, whether by private enterprise or the State, is as undemocratic as one-party rule in politics. There are certainly some wise and liberal employers, but the system is so liable to abuse (as we shall see) that it could never be tempered to solve all the problems created by the factional Management *versus* Labour, Worker *versus* Capitalist approach which, of itself, it can only foster.

The principles of *All Party Alliance,* applied to industry and commerce, can solve those problems as nothing else can even hope to do. In the form of *Alliance in Industry,* they can overcome what are today apparently insuperable ideological differences, and give to all sections of industry not only the incentive to work as a team, but a very real sense of their essential interdependence and common interest.

As with *All Party Alliance, Alliance in Industry* is evolutionary, easy to comprehend, and within easy reach.

Together, they meet beyond all argument the one supreme requirement of a true democracy: that justice to all not only be done, but is known to be done.

# BOOK II

## ALLIANCE IN INDUSTRY

Evolution to Industrial Democracy

# 6

Millions of British people once believed that nationalisation of an industry would bring industrial justice: 'fair play' for everyone involved. We now know that it brings simply a change of masters, and that the state is often a colder-blooded, more ruthless master than private enterprise.

There is no evidence that nationalisation is, or ever can be, a successful alternative or successor to private ownership.

Strikes and threats of strikes, lock-outs, restrictive practices, short time, low wages, and inefficiency, all these are as common in the nationalised industries as in those privately-owned. Moreover, all nationalised industries run at huge losses, thrusting heavy burdens on the taxpayer.*

Private ownership of industry, however, is becoming less and less successful. Under constant threat of take-over by near-monopolies or the state, constant threat of crippling strikes, and constant fear of being bled dry by taxation or strangled by lack of capital, the vitally important increase in our productivity is far too sluggish.

Leaders of industry, both private and state-owned, alike deplore this situation. For the most part extremely able, experienced men, they are astute enough to seek not only the

*For the sweeping reductions in taxation at all levels which *Alliance in Industry* will empower, see Chapter 9.

utmost possible productivity, but the most attractive possible pay and conditions for their employees.

Trades Union leaders, with few exceptions, want exactly the same things, for they are equally aware of the vital importance of high productivity and a successful industrial relations policy to sustained economic growth.

Yet the two groups are continually at loggerheads. At times, indeed, both seem more intent on 'scoring' against each other than in forging the unity which should be their most urgent concern.

The truth is that our productivity ratio is dangerously low because British industry (as well as British politics) consists of two bitterly opposing factions. These are management (with Capital) and Labour. In the prevailing atmosphere, new technological advances cannot even begin to realise their potential effect on output. Instead of welcoming the relief from drudgery and the inevitably shorter working week and greater leisure that automation and new techniques must eventually ensure (and basing their productivity agreements on those grounds), far too often the worker (Union) reaction to innovation is the suspicious hostility which management (Capital) has sourly come to expect.

Because just as the workers believe themselves cheated, victimised and exploited, so do the employers, who are convinced that the workers don't and won't do a fair day's work for a fair day's pay. With our competitor nations constantly seeking, and using, new and better methods of production, this hostility is not only wasteful but economically disastrous.

Together, British management and labour could be using their combined ideas, experience and unbeatable know-how, to make every new technique work to their fullest advantage, by both the swift expansion of existing industries and the establishment of new. But instead of uniting to fight off our competitor nations, the two sides waste a fantastic amount of time and energy in fighting each other.

Obviously, then, our present system of ownership and control can only continue to foster the 'Them versus us' approach which today splits all those involved in industry* into hostile camps. Our present industrial system unquestionably possesses exactly the same fundamental weakness as our present political system.

Both actually CREATE this conflict of interests—despite the fact that the interests of all concerned, whether in politics or in industry, are in essence inseparable.

A permanent end to this senseless conflict must be made, if we hope to evoke the unity we assuredly need to achieve a fully prosperous and continually-expanding economy.

The many previous attempts to find a solution have all proved abortive. The Labour Government's Prices and Incomes Policy—not to mention Mrs. Castle's "In Place of Strife"— simply revealed the conflict between the government and the Trade Unions at its stubborn worst.

But by the same token, when the Labour Party's manifesto on industrial democracy—which was supported by most Trade Unions—was first presented, it was just as sharply attacked by leaders of industry, through the Confederation of British Industries as well as by leading Conservatives. Worse: the attack was made before the C.B.I. could possibly have studied the manifesto.

The inescapable truth is that, under the existing system, the interests of the two main groups in industry and commerce do conflict and can never be more than temporarily reconciled.

*For 'industry', wherever applicable, read 'industry and commerce'.

This conflict can only be ended by a fundamental change away from our present system.

In Great Britain, we had a golden opportunity to make the change during the Industrial Revolution of the 1800s. Yet even such great social reformers as the Earl of Shaftesbury and Charles Dickens were so completely inured to the idea of private-owner control that they saw only the need for change in the gross abuses the system permitted, not in the system itself.

The profit-sharing and pension schemes of the early 1900s, radically progressive for their time, suffered equally from this unquestioned assumption of the need to operate within a system which made absolute justice for all utterly impossible.

Even in present-day Britain, the concept of single-ownership will undoubtedly die hard in some quarters. Nevertheless proposals for really imaginative, just, and wholly practicable reform must obviously fall on far more fertile ground today than would have been possible even as recently as five and ten years ago. Since the war, millions of men and women from every stratum of our society, deeply disturbed by the permanent economic threat both to the individual and to the nation inherent in monopoly of industry by private enterprise, have at some time actively supported the Great Experiment in State ownership and control.

*Nationalisation—100% state ownership and control—had to be tried for all their sakes.*

Today, with nationalisation proved such a palpable and staggeringly costly failure, those disenchanted millions are beginning to recognise that the basic fault lies in *the intrinsically-divisive concept of single-control and ownership, no matter by whom.*

What is needed most urgently is a system which not only

removes the causes of conflict, but so demonstrably establishes interdependence that it forges the unity which brings out the best in every group and individual involved. To do this, it must obviously evoke a sense of keen personal participation, and unquestioned assurance of absolute justice.

It is unrealistic to teach the child of his democratic heritage, the inalienable rights of man and then expect the adult willingly to forego his parliamentary right to true representation or to forfeit his waking day to another's whim. No man can ever feel justly treated if his livelihood is at constant hazard from the economic consequences of industrial policies in which he has had no voice.

*The total interdependence of all sections of industry, and thus the importance of every individual's contribution to its effective working, is unarguable.*

Once we recognise that simple truth, we cannot fail to recognise also that justice and human dignity actively demand that every man should share in the decisions, the over-all policy, and the fortunes—good or bad—of the business he serves. To put his best into his job, to care, and so to strive for his firm's greatest possible success, he must have a sense of belonging: of being an integral part of the company in his own right.

It is the absence of this sense of essential involvement which is the basic cause of so much dissatisfaction among employees, no matter how well-paid. However subconsciously in some, this deep need of the greatest incentive of all to personal endeavour is innate in everyone; all need a voice in their own destiny and a stake in their own achievement.

The many who believed this sense of full involvement would come with nationalisation of all the means of manufacture, distribution and supply, have been sadly disillusioned by the actuality of state-owned industry in operation. In their revulsion from the realities of state ownership and control, however, they have lost none of their antagonism to the remembered realities of total ownership and control by private enterprise. The fact is that requisite in both is a basic acceptance of an almost feudally autocratic 'Master and Man' relationship, which not only has no place in a democracy but is the greatest single barrier to industrial efficiency.

Whether in the West (chiefly by private enterprise) or in Communist countries (by the state), the longer single-ownership and control continues, the more self-evident its weaknesses and inevitable failure will become.

Again, there is a clear parallel with our present political system.

In this second half of the 20th century, single control and ownership of industry and commerce has failed and is failing. Just as single control and domination of a nation by one party contains, within itself, the seeds of its own destruction, so does single control of industry. Marx, when stating this principle in relation to Capitalism, did not realise that it would apply equally to Communism—since Communism (like nationalisation) is simply state capitalism.

Obviously, then, the needed change has to be within the structure of industrial and commercial ownership. Such a change to a system guaranteeing fair play and true rewards to all, could be introduced at very short notice, like its political counterpart, and its benefits would very swiftly begin to take effect.

Moreover, its very cognisance of the utter interdependence of every individual and every group involved, would weld now hostile factions into a team the world would find very hard to beat.

# 7

LABOUR FOR DEMOCRACY

this point is very largely out for the past year...
ground to defend its own position by dialectical warfare
mainly in the interests of its own advantage. Both the
older distributive parties, Tory, Liberal and Socialist, or
at least their left-wing and its leaders of little property
if it wanted to give up the idea to find that they
are too closely to limit even their land and socialist
thought, is not the distinct spirit of the official is
socially and both of its that its idea of interest so the...

In our present system of ownership and control of industry in general, there are two obvious groups involved: the labour force and management. Behind the labour force obviously stand the Trade Unions; and behind management stand the capitalists, whether private or state.

Since industry cannot exist if deprived of any one of these factors (Men, Money or Management), their identity of interest and so the need for mutual respect and trust between all three, is beyond question. Yet countless politicians on either 'side' are still guilty of a major crime in deliberately working on the fears and prejudices of their supporters so as to foster the antagonism and distrust which bedevils Britain's industrial relations.

It has suited Labour politicians to present the capitalist as a heartless ogre, cold-bloodedly intent on extracting the highest possible profit from his investment, at whatever cost or injustice to the worker. And it has suited Conservative politicians to present Trade Union leaders and lesser officials as largely Communist agitators and fellow-travellers, cold-bloodedly bent on creating strikes and unrest and restrictive practices so as to wreck Britain's economy, or at best hold management (and the capitalist) to financial ransom.

It has to be admitted that these are accurate enough

descriptions of a few on each side, but for the most part, they provide a deliberately and grotesquely distorted picture —purely in the interests of factional advantage. Each 'side', like the political parties, thus blames the other for productivity failures and the parlous state of the economy. Consequently each side is blinded to the fact that their interests are inseparable from each other's and the nation's.

There are in fact four distinct bodies or groups involved in industry, and today they share identity of interest as follows:

1. Labour Force and Trade Unions
2. Management, Research and Marketing
3. The Private Investor
4. The State.

Obviously no one group can function alone; each is an integral part of a whole. If one fails in its obligations, the others suffer. If outside influences (e.g. change of government or government policy, increased taxation, a 'wage freeze') impair one group's efficiency or morale, then all four groups suffer.

Whether a company is private- or state-owned, all the bodies involved are totally interdependent: no one group can, therefore, be of more or less importance than the next. And since industrial and commercial success are vital to our national prosperity, responsibility for the state of the economy thus devolves, in equal measure, upon all groups involved.

If all concerned must share that responsibility, then it follows that all concerned must, in simple justice, share the rewards.

Since single-ownership and control clearly cannot provide

this essential justice, the alternative can only be shared ownership and control. And justice could only be assured if all four groups concerned in, and so responsible for, the functioning of industry, had equal share—or 25% each.

As with *All Party Alliance, Alliance in Industry* is based on two essential democratic needs: (i) that of justice—'fair play' for all concerned, and (ii) the guarantee that no one group or faction could ever have power to usurp the authority of any other.

*In other words: as with the new political system, the new industrial system would make dictatorial control, by ANY group or ANY individual, completely impossible for all time.*

The mutual trust and respect these conditions would ensure between all groups and invididuals would provide a tremendous stimulus to active mutual concern for success. At the same time the reliable and increasing return on investment inevitable in a thriving, trouble-free industry, would benefit not only the capitalist but the labour force, management, and (through the State's 25% holding) the whole nation. But before looking at the effect of *Alliance in Industry* on each group, and the almost incalculable benefits to society and the nation as a whole, let us consider the problems of such a transfer of ownership.

There is, of course, ample precedent for complete change of ownership and control, in private and public undertakings.

In the nationalised industries, ownership is transferred, 100% overnight. True, certain preparations have been made in advance, and in most cases the practical management (as distinct from direction and control at boardroom level) remains virtually the same. So whatever the long-term effects of nationalisation, the actual change-over is in no way disruptive. There is no immediately noticeable effect on the workers, or on the running of the industry and the firms which comprise it.

With *Alliance in Industry,* however, hitherto untried factors would be introduced.

Workers would become entitled to a share of control at boardroom level, where their elected representatives would generally lack experience. On the other hand, their specialised knowledge of the worker and his work, like the new and deeper insight they would gain into problems of management, marketing and finance, would be of inestimable value in removing misunderstanding and establishing mutual trust and respect between management and men.

Then again, the workers would be shareholders; but many would have no idea how to benefit from their holdings. (It is just this lack of experience which has led, in the past, to abuses of schemes run by individual companies—and thus to the claim, often made, that workers don't want shares.)* Much the same is true of the low-salaried white-collar worker. Each of these groups would have to learn how to make their newly-acquired shares 'work' for them: how to take the best possible advantage of a very real stake in their own present and future prosperity.

The private investor, too, would need time to adjust to the change.

Today, practically every industry, individual company or corporation, whether private- or state-owned, is 100% so owned. Since under *Alliance in Industry* no owner could retain more than 25% in any one Company, all present owners would have to sell or otherwise divest themselves of 75% of their holdings.†

The 75% withdrawn from state undertakings would of

*See Chapter 8.

†Various forms of compensation and re-investment are discussed in detail in the next two chapters.

course be re-invested in those where the state at present has no holding. But the big individual or group private investors required to take 75% of their capital out of each firm, must have time to decide how to re-invest it. In any case, no industry could withstand the shock of sudden withdrawal of 75% of the capital invested in it, for this could not be immediately replaced by the purchaser, as happens when industries are nationalised.

So the transition would have to be gradual: spread evenly over five years at least, or possibly ten. In this way, each industry and each firm could absorb and adjust to the changes, without loss or disruption.

Obviously, then, *Alliance in Industry* is not put forward as an 'instant' panacea for industry's (and so the economy's) ills. It is a considered and gradual change from one group of investors to four different groups which have identical interests, to make the industry as efficient and successful as it can possibly be.

To understand how the system would work, it is necessary to examine each of the groups, separately and in relation to each other. Only thus can we see the natural evolutionary progression which must inevitably lead to *Alliance in Industry*. Only thus can we hope fully to comprehend the interdependence of each group. And only thus can we show the enormous benefit each group would derive.

# 8

If workers should suddenly become shareholders in an industry, and as suddenly have a share in its control, how would they cope?

Even a few years ago, that question would have spotlighted a valid weakness. Today, however, the private investor is no longer necessarily an individual who holds most of the purse-strings. He is often a working-man, or one of modest independent means. As often, he is self-employed: doctor, lawyer, accountant and the like, and his investments may amount to anything from a few pounds to a few thousand.

Whilst some extremely wealthy individuals and companies still can and do invest heavily, the small investor is playing an increasingly significant part in the capitalisation of industry. These comparatively small capitalists invest mostly in three different ways: gilt-edged, commercial and industrial stocks, and through Unit Trusts. These trusts have expanded enormously in the last few years. They take the capital from hundreds of small investors and spread the combined investments over a wide range of British industrial and commercial stocks, as well as judiciously-selected overseas stocks.

The actual trust investor has little or nothing to do, perhaps less to worry about. Everything is done for him by experts, and in the vast majority of cases he gets a sound yield from his investment.

Under *Alliance in Industry* this principle would be applied to all employees, whether on the factory floor, at managerial, research or marketing level. Their capital would be handled for them: they need only become actively involved in deciding what to do with their dividends. And all workers, both skilled and unskilled, would be (individually):

1. Allotted shares according to length of service in the company.
2. Allotted shares as a bonus for increased productivity.
3. Permitted to take shares as part of their wages.
4. Encouraged to buy shares through the special schemes, out of their savings.

The Trades Unions, of course, are for the most part already big private investors—that is, capitalists—in their own right. (In itself, this is a giant stride forward from the old Socialist portrayal of every capitalist as an exploiter of human misery, living by the sweat of other men's brows!)

Many Trade Unions, moreover, have large holdings in gilt-edged as well as in speculative shares. Many, of course, invest in Unit Trusts, and there would be no need for them to change their present investment habits: Trade Union capital is, after all, derived mainly from fees or dues of members and obviously should be invested so as to give the utmost benefit to those members. The only condition (which would be strictly applied) would be that the total shares owned by the Unions and labour-force between them must not exceed 25% of the capital investment in any one firm or enterprise.

The Trades Unions' interest, however, would spread much

further. For many years they have been seeking representation on the boards of many industries, and the chief objection has always been that they are not shareholders. With *Alliance in Industry,* however, they could be shareholders in their own right, and as shareholders they would be entitled to representation on the relevant boards in proportion to their holdings. Save for the hopeless hostility between so many Unions today, they would also be the obvious choice to represent the workers in the boardroom.

What would happen if they were to amalgamate so as to regroup themselves (as eventually they surely must) and divide not by trade, but by industry, so that the whole labour-force in each separate firm was represented by one specific Union?

*The relevant Unions would (subject to the approval of the workers concerned) have an equal right with management, capital, and the state, to 25% of the seats on every board in their industry.*

The value of this basically simple change from our present hopelessly archaic approach to the problems of industry cannot be overstated. It would send a refreshing and long overdue blast of sanity and mutual enlightenment through the barriers of utterly artificial, senselessly partisan, blindly self-destructive hostility and distrust which pass as 'industrial relations' in Britain today.

The Unions' task would no longer be to conduct a continuous battle, on their members' behalf, against employers and management. It would be to thrash out, *with* them, the surest and swiftest way to achieve the highest possible profits and the widest possible markets, so that their members (the workers) would at last be seeing concrete—and continuing—returns for their efforts, in the form of healthy dividends.

No excuse or reason would remain for the Unions to create

restrictive practices. Since strikes, wildcat or otherwise, could only harm the worker-shareholder's own interests, strikes would soon become a thing of the past. Grievances and misunderstandings would be aired and ironed out at boardroom level, among equals—with equal interest in maintaining unity, by ensuring 'fair play' for *all*.

*Alliance in Industry,* in short, guarantees what no other system of industrial relationship can even hope to offer: to preserve for all time the *right* to strike, but remove for all time the *need*.

The unarguable justice of such a new system—the obvious benefit to be derived by every worker and by the Unions themselves—is so evident that, once having comprehended the full significance of the proposed change, all but the most diehard Socialist or Conservative would surely quickly come to welcome it.

The Unions' task of looking after the interests of the workers would remain as important as ever. They would keep welfare, wages and working conditions, holidays, privileges and rights, under constant survey, just as they do today. But they would know that for their members themselves to reap the highest possible rewards, the business must prosper; so productivity at the keenest possible price would be the basis on which they operated.

Can anyone doubt that the system itself would ensure good Labour-Management relations? Or that every worker would have a far better deal than he has today, a sense of absolute justice, and every conceivable incentive to put his very best efforts into his job? The odd 'rogue' employee might attempt to slack, of course, but since even one man not pulling his weight would slow down the over-all effort—thus cheating every other worker—the Unions would undoubtedly find ways to ensure that each man did his job with reasonable responsibility.

The genuine low-geared workers (those having, for various unavoidable reasons, a lower-output capacity) could be fitted without real or imagined hardship into jobs where their restricted tempo would have the least possible braking effect on the general productivity, simply because under the new system, the levelling would be *up*—not down, as it usually is today. Allocation of the most highly-productive, and so best-paid, jobs would no longer be a matter for jealousy or 'demarcation' squabbles. The new system really would inevitably engender a true 'team spirit'. Since every man would benefit from the over-all achievement—since every dividend would be the higher for increased productivity—everyone would feel active concern to see that every job went to the best possible man to fill it.

Obviously, then, the Unions and their members would have 100% incentive to achieve maximum efficiency, and thus maximum profit.

As obviously, management (administration/sales/research staff) would, individually, be:

1. Allotted shares according to length of service in the company.
2. Allotted shares as bonus for increased efficiency and profit.
3. Permitted to take shares in lieu of salary.
4. Encouraged to buy shares through the special schemes provided.

Moreover, management would find itself in a position of strength and confidence it has never known: freed, at last, of the three major handicaps under which it has laboured for far too long:

1. The constant fear or fact of strikes and restrictive practices which have wrecked or endangered production schedules and, in most areas of industry, have made full productivity virtually impossible.
2. The 'brain drain'—the excessive loss of technicians and research-workers to the U.S.A., Canada, Australia and other nations.
3. Lack of capital investment, necessitating the use of outdated and often outworn machinery and methods.

With *Alliance in Industry,* as we have already seen, the major cause of strikes and restrictive practices would be removed. And the cure for the brain drain is also inherent in the system. Since research staff would have a wholly fair personal share in their firm's prosperity, and since a prosperous industry would naturally have more money to spare for research—and up-to-date equipment—they would no longer feel that their efforts were wasted or ill-rewarded. They would have every incentive to stay in Britain, as most would much prefer. Today, they are driven away by conditions at home and lured by the considerably greater scope—and salaries—their qualifications ensure abroad.

The *need* for incentives to keep them here is far more important than is generally realised. In the realms of technological research particularly, Britain very often leads the world. An enthusiastic research and design force will be spurred on by the knowledge that they are personally playing an active, fully appreciated, and truly rewarding part in building the brighter future and better society they desire.

Strong and healthy prestige-building competition with our rival nations would replace the resigned and apathetic approach all too prevalent today.

As to the third major handicap, the next chapter will show how *Alliance in Industry* would release almost unlimited capital for investment. It will also show why I believe the new system to be the only way to ensure drastic reductions in the scandalously high rate of personal taxation—the greatest of all disincentives to endeavour, at every level—*for every taxpayer*, in industry and out.

Just as management and research staff of all companies will benefit very greatly, so will the sales staff. Given the certainty of competitively-priced goods and reliable delivery dates, as well as a fair share of the profits from their own efforts, they would have the confidence and the compelling incentive to enlarge and extend their markets.

So, as with the labour-force, everyone in management would identify themselves with, and have a fair share in, the firm itself—and in the profits made. Since the success of each firm would thus be of vital importance to every individual in it, with personal as well as team effort made truly rewarding in every sense, can it be doubted that productivity would rise on a dramatic scale?

The opportunity for Britain to adopt and operate such a predictably popular and unarguably practical system could hardly come at a better moment. The world-wide demand both for higher standards of living and for 'consumer goods'—ranging anywhere from food and clothing, medical supplies and household equipment, to aircraft and ships, farm and industrial machinery—has never been greater. Even in the U.S.A. and here in Britain, there are still huge pockets of citizens living at or below minimum standards of subsistence.

In other Western nations, such pockets of under-privileged are much greater; while in Asia, the Middle East, Southern Europe, South America, Russia, China and the whole of the Far East, the masses live at an abysmally low standard.

Since practically everything needed to raise the standard of living is consumable—that is, can be eaten, drunk, used up, or worn out—world production can never, within any remotely calculable time, catch up with world demand. But the vast potential consumer-market of the 'have-not' nations cannot be realised without the practical help, in the first instance, of the 'haves'.

As productivity increases in Britain, it follows that the national economy will prosper. With a prospering national economy, it will be easier to give credit to the emergent nations. This will enable them to buy more and more goods—including more and more industrial plants and machines. With these, they will be able to achieve a standard of living which will in turn increase consumer demand for more and more goods.

An ascending scale of prosperity, of living standards and consumer goods-consumption is absolutely inevitable throughout the world, and Britain needs only a fair share of this to ensure that she reaches the coming Age of Leisure as soon as any other nation. Thus, the initial assistance provided by Britain and other 'have' nations would prove to be, in fact, a most practical long-term form of economic 'self-help'.

However, nothing approaching the prosperity we need even to assure a reasonably good and improving standard of living for every person in Britain itself, is possible with the existing system of single ownership and control.

*And as with All Party Alliance, the transition to Alliance in Industry could begin AT ONCE.*

# 9

The two capitalist bodies or groups in Great Britain are the state, which derives its income almost exclusively from taxation, and the industrialist/banker/private investor, whose income is derived in one form or another from profits in trading.

It has long been commonly accepted that these two groups are bitterly hostile to each other: that the state *versus* capitalism is a natural alignment. If this were true it would in effect mean a never-ending war of capitalism *versus* capitalism. In truth, however, the conflict between the two is as artificial as that between worker and management. It is fundamentally unrealistic and economically suicidal, for neither form of capitalism can ever defeat the other without in the long run harming itself. As with politics, so with capitalism, so with industry: any system which permits and perpetuates such internecine strife is inherently bad and self-destructive.

The deliberately-fostered ideological conflict between Socialism and Conservatism, equated by many with state *versus* private enterprise, has obscured the real truth for far too long. *Worse: it has blinded us to the interdependence of us all, whatever our age, financial position, or walk of life.*

State ownership should be seen for what it is: simply a variation in the source of capital used in production.

Let us examine more closely what would happen to private capital, under *Alliance in Industry*. We know that some of the 75% shareholding of which private investors must divest themselves would be given or otherwise allocated to the management and labour force. Normally, of course, there would be direct compensation, in cash or kind, to relieve the owners of any loss.

However, let us assume that 10% of all present capital investment were to be given, free (by private owners *and* the state) to be shared among all employees, in both management and labour sectors, in return (pro rata) for their years of service. And let us assume that in the case of the private shareholders, their investment today yields 10% in dividends.

If, as a result of the much greater productivity which the new system would ensure, the yield on capital investment went up even to 11¼%, then the private investor's remaining 90% would produce, in dividends, the same actual *money* as if he had retained the full 100% investment at today's rate. In that way, the investor's compensation would come through the improved productivity: it would involve no loss and no one would have to buy the 10% relinquished.

Over the period of transition (five to ten years), this process could be repeated as increased productivity allowed, until the shares acquired—given, bought, or earned as bonus—by both management and by the labour force, each totalled 25% of the whole.

Most of the private investors' present stake in industry would of course have to be sold—the process of giving could not be unlimited. So if the investor gave away 10% of his original 100% he would still have to sell 65%. Some of the money from this he would re-invest in a greater variety of firms and industries. He would spread his risks while at the same time making new capital available for the expansion of our many gravely under-capitalised industries.*

Moreover, some of this freed capital could and should be invested overseas, starting with soft-currency areas. This would achieve what is today the near-impossible: it would increase our invisible exports, in the form of dividends on these new investments. Britain's trading position would be greatly improved in this way, also, and with it, our balance of payments situation given even greater strength. Sterling would once again be hard currency.

So, simply by changing from an inherently-divisive (and economically sterile) system to one which has unity inherent within it, we should have established the flourishing economy we all seek. It cannot be said too often that this is possible only with the active co-operation of everyone involved, plus the proof, in hard cash, of a justified faith in our ability to do so. This proof would be in the form of monetary backing from:

1. Savings (invested income) of the labour force and management.
2. The increased yield on capital already invested at home.
3. Profits on the new overseas investments.

In short, the new capital—and the nation's new prosperity—would come out of *the greater productivity which Alliance in Industry, in operation, cannot fail to create*.

We come now to the last investor: the state.

*Most of the capital which would change hands would be handled through the Stock Exchange, as it is today. Employees and the Unions would buy some shares and the state would buy up to 25% of the total (but *never* more).

Clearly, over the transition period, the state would have to sell its remaining 65% of all nationalised industries back to private enterprise (including 25% direct to non-employee investors). The gradual return of the nationalised industries to largely private ownership and control would give the believer in capitalism a tremendous opportunity to prove that power, the docks, shipping, shipbuilding, air lines, railways, telephone services and even the mines could be run at a profit. The prospect of profit to themselves would give back to both workers and management the incentive to effort which nationalisation so signally fails to provide.

Meanwhile, over the same period the state would acquire 25% of *all* industry, and as we shall see, its 25% of the dividends would be of enormous benefit to *all* tax-payers. The private capital investor and the state would each have 25% of the total investment in all industry, the 50% being shared equally between workers and management. Only the most doctrinaire Capitalist-Conservatives or Labour Nationalisationists could ever desire to defend their old ideological concepts against the patent good sense, powerful incentives, and 'fair play' to all, which such a system would ensure.

Socialists would have what they have always wanted but can never achieve under the present system *or* under total state ownership (state capitalism) of all industry: absolute justice for *all involved* in industry and commerce.

Conservatives would have what they want: largely private ownership and control of the means of manufacture, distribution and supply—*and a previously undreamed-of degree of enthusiastic co-operation and goodwill from the work-force, the Unions, and every department of management.*

Who could complain? And, since both private enterprise and the state have already, separately, *proved* their inability to do remotely as well—how could any Socialist or Conservative ever again even claim that 'his' way would be better?

With labour-management relations no longer relatable to party-political issues, the old 'automatic' conflicts would be swiftly forgotten in the face of obvious common interest and mutual gain. Ideological differences could at last take their proper place in the reasoned discussion that alone can lead to intelligent adaptation and adoption of policies, from whatever source, which are demonstrably in the general interest.

Finally, we turn to those employed in the non-productive industries and trades, and non-profit making public services, such as hospital staff, civil servants and municipal employees.

In many of these sectors, 'streamlining' to achieve highest efficiency at lowest cost is today invariably restricted by unavoidable financial considerations. But there is no reason at all why a thriving industry should not, by common consent of those involved, make substantial contributions (before distribution of profits) to national health and welfare services. There is no reason why in towns which are largely dependent on a few major firms, these firms should not make such contributions to specific local undertakings which will benefit the whole community.

Moreover, there is no reason why a prosperous state should not meet some, if not all, of the present cost of these services to the individual. The state's purchase of its 25% ownership in industry would be spread over the five to ten years agreed transition period—so its annual investment would be comparatively small.

During that same period, it would be receiving payment for the 65% of now-nationalised undertakings remaining, after allocation of 10% to its employees. This payment, plus the dividends on its *new* investments, would in the main be set against (a) the purchase of the next year's share-buying and (b) taxation generally.

Now increasingly, as the transition from the present system to *Alliance in Industry* neared completion (and certainly once its full 25% holding in industry was achieved), the state would have an enormous profit with which to help pay for all civil, military and welfare services—and so relieve the burden on *every* tax-payer, right across the board.

*Even at today's by no means impressive distributed profits figures, 25% of these profits come to over £1,000 millions: that would cut about 3/-d in the pound off income tax.* And as distributed profits rose, so further reductions in forms of taxation would be possible.

It becomes apparent from these figures, surely irrefutable on close and unbiased study, that one of the basic fallacies of modern society is that a state must pay for its activities out of taxes. In fact *there is no need at all for high taxation,* for nations as well as giant corporations can and should be run at a profit. It is clearly true that personal income tax (which was introduced originally as a 'temporary measure') could and surely should be abolished at the earliest possible moment, and only surtax be retained, although even that at a far less punitive, incentive-killing rate than now.

Given a sufficiently thriving industry in an increasingly prosperous world, the yield in dividends from the state's 25% holdings could eventually offset the actual cost of running the country: at the very least, enough to abolish income tax. And any reduction in taxation, even one which could be made in the first year, would obviously be a tremendous incentive at every level.

The fall in taxation would free still more privately-owned

capital (as would the fact that shares could be accepted, at market prices, in lieu of taxes, in companies where the state would be acquiring an eventual 25% holding). It would allow the wage-earner and salaried employee to keep more of his pay-packet, or invest more in his own or other companies. It would enable taxes on industry and commerce to be reduced: again, freeing more money for investment. And lower taxation would be of direct and very welcome benefit to the retired as well as to others on fixed incomes.

A continually falling tax-rate would mean that, *instead of today's steady increase in taxation, there would be a rising spiral of income at all levels.*

Not only would this mean that we were making the nation pay for itself. We would literally *be* 'running Britain at a profit'—a profit which *all* would truly share.

It is, I repeat, within our reach; and it is well within our capabilities. Everything the world needs, after all, stems from just three things:

1. Raw materials.
2. Manpower.
3. Know-how.

There is virtually no limit to the supply of these three 'basics'. And there is no limit at all to the demand for what they are able to produce, of the right quality and at the right price. *All that has been missing is the incentive which can only be found in a system which will use these three 'basics' to proper advantage.*

No system could use them to better advantage than *Alliance in Industry,* with its fundamental incentives of fair play—and fair shares—for everyone involved.

# EVOLUTION TO DEMOCRACY

No other existing system even begins to offer such an honourable, unchallengeably just, and economically sound compromise between the rights and needs of what are, today, the so-senselessly-opposed 'sides' of industry—nor between the ideological aims of the parties which 'represent' them. *Only Alliance in Industry* can guarantee freedom from bullying, dictatorial control or ruinous, sterile restriction and strikes, which must forever remain a threat under single ownership, whether private *or* state.

Because to sum up, *with Alliance in Industry, ownership and commerce would be shared:*

25% by the TRADE UNIONS and the WORKERS, who back Britain with their energy, craftsmanship and skills . . . Problems would be thrashed out—and workers' rights protected—at boardroom level, by workers' own representatives . . . No need for strikes, lock-outs, restrictive practices . . . No one is going to strike against himself!

25% by MANAGEMENT, SALES and RESEARCH STAFF, who back Britain with their ideas, experience and know-how . . . Really powerful incentives to personal and team endeavour . . . really worthwhile rewards for achievement . . . No need for our 'brains' to leave home—every encouragement and opportunity, indeed, to stay and make Britain a place to be proud of.

25% by the PRIVATE INVESTORS, who back Britain and British workmanship with their own hard cash . . . No longer the Capitalist ogre-figure of Socialist teaching, the private investor would be seen for what he is: a partner, who deserves the certainty the new system would provide, of really worthwhile dividends on the money he risks.

25% by THE STATE—*to help pay for running the country* . . . The state would buy shares at market value . . . accept others as payment of taxes . . . Its share of the profits would slash taxes right across the board, yet leave more to spend on the Social Services.

*So, ALLIANCE IN INDUSTRY means:*

No need for strikes . . . for short time . . . for restrictive practices . . .

No need for suspicion . . . mistrust . . . futile hostility . . .

Workers, capitalists, management, 'back-room boys' and front-line salesmen, always working together, *because it pays them.*

It is worth noting that since I first submitted these proposals to leaders of industry and commerce, not one single individual has said: "It cannot be done." but many have said: 'Human nature being what it is, how will you ever get everyone to work together? How will you ever persuade the doctrinaire Socialist or the die-hard Capitalist to yield an inch?"

The point they have failed to grasp is that their objections are valid only in the light of conditions existing *today*, under single-ownership and control. Moreover, *already*, doctrinaire Socialists accept Union and worker involvement as capitalist-investors through Unit Trusts, etc. *Already*, doctrinaire Conservatives accept nationalisation—*100% state ownership*—in some industries and corporations (which the new system would not permit).

So the truth, I am convinced, is that as *all* those involved begin to see the benefits that they themselves will derive from *Alliance in Industry,* they will not only be 'ready to work together'—they will *demand* the transition, at the earliest possible time.

*For a start, they should demand that the change-over be made in three industries in obvious and urgent need of reform, which could serve as 'test' cases for the new system: the docks, shipbuilding, and steel.*

Only the people can demand these changes, of course, and I believe that as more and more come to realise the very great benefit these simple changes would bring, they will reject any politician who tries, even for a day, to hold back this evolutionary tide which will carry us to true democracy.

*Is there any other way* which offers even hope of a voluntary end to strikes and restrictive practices? To the 'brain drain'? *Any* other way which would even begin to achieve the kind of productivity ratios that this new system certainly would? Which could create the conditions and provide the capital for industrial expansion on every front? Which could increase the national income from invisible exports? And which could offer to *everyone in the land* the all-compelling incentive of reduced taxation, along with expanding and improved social services?

There are men of every income bracket, in industry and out, who believe *Alliance in Industry* to be 'the answer' for Britain. Some (chiefly capitalists and management) approve because they recognise the ever-present threat, under the present system, of total take-over by the state of any large and flourishing concern—with predictable damage to efficiency and profits—and applaud a system which would restrict its power. Others (chiefly Liberals and disillusioned Socialists) find in *Alliance in Industry* the justice, the respect for the working-man's real value, and the concrete incentives to effort so utterly lacking in both private and state-owned enterprise today.

Many more, from hard-headed businessmen to equally hard-headed industrial correspondents, simply regard this proposed system as the first-ever really viable plan for getting the economic results we so desperately need, without the offensive, embittering and above all, *ineffectual* threats of penalties—and thus of equally embittering and futile strikes.

*The truth is that all other possibilities have been tried, and have failed, whereas Alliance in Industry, with all its obvious benefits to the individual and the nation, is within easy reach.*

Only the obstinate prejudices of the two main political parties, and of their too-long 'blinkered' Big Business and organised labour followers, prevents us from moving *at once* towards this great industrial evolution.

# 10

I have no fear that bigotry, intellectual blindness, or deliberately-fostered antagonism will long stay the adoption of *All Party Alliance.* History has taught that the mind of man is illimitably flexible. However ingrained the old fallacy, the old misteaching, once the truth lodges in man's mind it is ineradicable. And in a free society, the inalienable rights of man are a fact of life—a truth, of all truths, worth defending.

In Britain, social and political justice for all is not a privilege, but our right. I believe that as more and more people see the justice, and the strength, of *All Party Alliance,* they will be satisfied with nothing less.

This outline of the principles and proposals has been written chiefly with reference to political and industrial conditions in Britain. But the general principles can be adapted with comparative ease to strengthen other forms of democracy, not least in those nations where proper democratic safeguards are even more urgently needed than in Britain. Most of the African states which have emerged from colonial rule in the past twenty-five years, and would much prefer to pride themselves on the democratic ethos they so confidently foresaw, find themselves instead in acute danger of dictatorship.

The claim that such countries need a strong man to lead

and build them is true enough. But *all* countries need outstanding men at the helm, just as all countries flourish best in freedom. Only men of great stature can work with the day-by-day scrutiny and approval of all shades of political opinion; but those who can are in fact the strongest men of all.

Indeed, no Prime Minister, whether of a new country or an old, could be blind to the tremendous national and international prestige involved in leading a Cabinet of truly outstanding men. And what system, other than *All Party Alliance,* could *allow* such a man office, without fear of *creating* dictatorship?

Even in the older nations, present forms of democracy have worn very thin and the need for a new basis of government is becoming obvious.

Switzerland, and some Scandinavian countries where the systems of government are not too far removed, in principle, from *All Party Alliance,* would obviously find it very easy—and greatly to their advantage—to adapt. But even for a nation like Yugoslavia, a gradual progression to *All Party Alliance* is by no means unthinkable. Between the more liberal Communist thinking and the A.P.A. concept there is nothing like the vast gulf that exists between doctrinaire Communism and 100% Western capitalism today.

Indeed, *All Party Alliance,* in both its political and industrial forms, could well be the meeting-ground between East and West; between now obdurately-opposed ideologies which—if the world is to find true peace, and man true happiness—*must* one day merge in a *modus vivendi* acceptable to all.

During the American Presidential election campaign in 1968, I drove through half the United States; listening to radio, watching television, reading newspapers, talking to as many people as I could. Everywhere, without exception, there was weariness with the party conflict. Everywhere, people called almost in desperation for unity. Huge advertisements appeared on hoardings, in the press and on television and radio, urging each elector to vote for the man best suited for the job; *not* for his party.

Sponsored by Committees for Independent Action, these groups often supported simultaneously, for instance, a Republican for the U.S. Senate, a Democrat for Congress, and an Independent for State Senator. In New York, during the last hectic days of the campaign, there were powerful calls to vote for the *man*, not for the party.

*The fact that, throughout the country, there were people prepared to back with hard cash their pleas for men in public office who would put the best interests of all the people before any party, is one of the healthiest and most significant phenomena in American society today.*

I believe that these men are simply the active, articulate tip of a nation-wide iceberg. That they reflect not only the increasing repugnance for 'power politics' at every level, but also a very deep concern at the internal strife which so ravages the nation at home, and besmirches its image abroad. And obviously, as more and more come to realise that the political *system* actively fosters the seething resentment and frustration which all too often boils over into violent protests, they, too, will be urgently seeking a system which will bring out the best in all party politicians and their leaders.

The American practice of giving office to Democrats in a Republican administration and *vice versa,* is closer than the British system to the spirit and concept of *All Party Alliance.* The American system still splits the country into bitterly opposing camps, however, and Americans in general regard state participation in industry with abhorrence. Socialism, to most of them—and even Liberalism, to many—is so very closely related to Communism, that anything which even might be related is immediately rejected.

*All Party Alliance* and *Alliance in Industry*, however, between them would make nationalisation, as well as dictatorship, completely impossible, while at the same time ensuring a visibly better social and political deal for everyone. Once the American people, politicians, industrialists and capitalists realise this, they may well turn towards it with their usual tremendous, whole-hearted vigour and dedication.

For if ever a nation were wholeheartedly dedicated to the spirit of democracy, it is the United States of America.

Already in the U.S.A. today, there are great corporations which operate in the awareness and on the principle of interdependence and mutual interest: giving shares to their workers and consciously setting out to instil in *every* employee, from doorman to top management, a sense of personal involvement in the company's affairs. Naturally, they are astonished and bitterly disappointed when they, too, have labour troubles in common with less progressive firms.

"Will nothing satisfy them?" they cry.

The answer is simple: "Yes; the workers will be satisfied the moment they know that the society in which they live is truly just. Piecemeal justice will never satisfy them, because they know that what is given the lucky few as a privilege should be available to *all,* by right."

The reason for so much 'biting of the hand that feeds them' is that the 'Them *versus* Us' mentality has been fostered too deliberately and too long: is too deeply-ingrained to succumb to particular or minority favour. As long as there is injustice to one, justice to all is in danger.

Too many financiers and leaders of industry still pay only lip-service to democracy. Yet it is these men, with their exceptional brains and business acumen, who—if they pause to consider—will see more clearly than any, the infinitely greater scope for expansion (and vastly improved returns on investment) that *Alliance in Industry* guarantees.

*And it is just these men who are likeliest to become the cornerstone of this new system, this blueprint for industrial unity founded on true democratic realism.*

We have come to think of 'realism' as something less than the best: as 'the best attainable'. Time and time again, in modern history, a so-called 'realistic' policy has meant a compromise between good policy and bad. In desperate efforts to make a worn-out system work, industrial as well as social policies have also been approached with this false realism.

"We must," say such self-styled realists, "cut our coat according to our cloth." And: "Politics is the art of the possible."

Acceptance of these cliches *has led the world to two global wars, Nazism, Communism, Capitalism, the slaughter of the Jews, the bitter 'cold war' between East and West, the universal fear of nuclear weapons, a world divided into Haves and Have-nots, famine and squalor for hundreds of millions of people, massive corruption in high places, and political and international emnities without number.*

Socially, it has led to almost unbelievable inequalities in nations with a high standard of living, to slaughter on the roads, crime on an unprecedented scale, widespread toleration of customs and other tax evasion, and a general deterioration of integrity.

In Great Britain, there is a growing sense of cynicism: more and more people give less and less value in work and in service to one another and to the community. Discourtesy and incivility are on the increase. Youth has no leadership, no guidance, no sense of participation or of common purpose. Disunity and disillusion is rife: not only is the country divided into hostile camps, but each camp is bitterly divided within itself. Worse still, as the economy becomes weaker and weaker—inevitable in a divided nation—the cost in direct and indirect taxation to the individual becomes higher and higher.

There is widespread frustration and anger at the arbitrary conduct of the nation's leaders and their flagrant disregard of the public will. Those who did *not* vote Labour in 1966—that is, the great majority of the voting public—resented the government from the start. Those who did vote Labour were for the most part deeply disillusioned and resentful, two or three short years later. Yet what redress had any of them against an increasingly unrepresentative government which could cynically persist in pursuing—in all their names—policies with which they totally disagreed?

The truth is that the British people are never consulted enough.

Who ever bothered to ask how people felt about Capital Punishment? About the Divorce Laws? Immigration? Anguilla? Biafra? Rhodesia? Vietnam? The Common Market? Or any number of other, equally vital issues?

*I say that public opinion should be canvassed at least once a year, on every issue on which there is serious public controversy.*

The cost would be negligible.

We should simply hold a National Referendum along with the nation-wide annual Council elections. *All it would need is ONE extra ballot-box at each polling-booth and TWO ballot-papers instead of one.* (White paper for the vote, coloured for the Referendum.)

Government, whether local or national, cannot after all be by the people and for the people *unless* the community's and the nation's leaders know what the people want. The widespread conviction that nobody in authority *wants* to know is one of the root causes of the deplorably low polls in both local and national elections.

But there is a growing tendency at Council elections at least, to vote for the man, *not* the party. This is a heartening indication of developing public realisation that it is indefensible for decisions affecting *all* our lives to be made by the Party Whip.

Equally encouraging is the fact that throughout the country, thoughtful city and town councillors are beginning to opt out of the party war. Retiring chairmen, protected whilst in office from party dictate or pressure, are becoming increasingly unready to discard their impartial approach to community problems along with the tenure of office. The proportion of independent candidates for Council office, too, has shown a marked increase.

As more and more see the simple justice—and common sense—of making their decisions in the light of existing circumstances and *the ratepayers' wishes,* rather than party interest or advantage, more and more will follow suit. When every elector can be assured that once in the polling-booth he can have an effective voice in the national issues of the day as well as the chance to vote for a man no Whip will be allowed to silence, the present high rate of abstentions will be a thing of the past.

On the political realism of *All Party Alliance,* all the rest can be built. For, true realism can only lie in making the most intelligent possible use of the means and minds of men, to ensure the highest possible best out of life for us all. The size of the cloth from which we cut our coats will be exactly as 'limitable' as the mind of man. Because politics is as much the art of living as the art of government, while *reason* to hope, *chance* to achieve, *certainty* of the attainable better, is the ideal that all men seek even though our present system appears to make it an impossible dream.

Realism and idealism, then, can now be seen for what they are: identical twins, equally and interdependently essential to the freedom and happiness of all mankind.

I am sure that, with the rest of the democratic world, we have reached a point in human evolution at which another wrong turning from the path to true political social justice could prove disastrous.

So many people, today, are victims of the injustice so ironically inherent in the system man has created in his search for justice, or allowed, by negligence, to create itself. Continued refusal to meet reality with flexibility and compassion could at any time spark long-standing grievance and resentment into bitter revolt against society as we know it.

In Britain, the state of the economy alone is proof enough that we are living on borrowed time. But there is enough time, if only the holders of power and public office will open their eyes and see.

*Or if all those who do see will just use their votes, and their voices, to tell them what the people say must be done.*

# SUMMATION

by

Olga Stringfellow

# SUMMATION

by

Olga Stringfellow

I first met John Creasey at a writers' summer school in Derbyshire, where he was speaking on the social consequences of crime-writing: in essence, the unobtrusive establishing of standards of right and wrong, good and evil which, he reasoned, make the good crime novel the morality play of our time. And where I, when it came my turn to speak, found myself facing accusations of too much realism in my writings—and a too-idealistic concept of human relations.

As I protested, baffled, that in any balanced approach to human existence, idealism and realism were surely inseparable, the broadest beam of approval came from this man whose whole philosophy of life is based on that one conviction.

For to John Creasey, as I soon learned, idealism and realism are not only essentially inseparable but inseparably essential to the freedom and happiness of all mankind. And with no knowledge that this unshakable belief had driven him all his life to fight for a better political and social deal for his fellow-men, but at least in the certainty that here was someone who would care, I poured out to him all my own despair and alarm at what was happening to Britain at the hands of the political parties.

I was appalled by the immaturity and shocking self-interest

131

of their approach to the nation's affairs, the corrosive effect of their constant jockeying for position on individual and collective parliamentary integrity, the slavish obedience accorded the Party Whips, the dangerous shift of parliamentary power to a handful of party bosses, the mounting and all too understandable public distrust of the government and of politicians generally, and above all, the apparent blind indifference of every party to the economic madness of the system they uphold.

Parliamentary democracy—representative government—has been replaced in Britain by a system of alternating neo-dictatorships, led by party hard-liners who would uphold to a man Disraeli's outrageous retort to Bulwer Lytton: 'Damn your principles! Stick to your party!' To which, nevertheless, the only possible response of sane and honest men must surely be an emphatic: 'Damn your *party*! Stick to your principles!'

There is no conceivable case to be made for those in public office who would put personal or party interests before the nation's: still less for any who would command that others do so. It seemed to me insane that we should let this travesty of democratic process continue; yet short of filling the House with provenly public-spirited independents, I could see no way out. And while admittedly independents could not be coerced by promise of party patronage or threat of party rejection, they would have no collective aims or policies on which to seek electoral support.

Angered and depressed by it all for so long, I was hardly optimistic when John Creasey said a quiet: "I think I may have an answer." Then proceeded to outline to me not just *an* answer, but what I knew beyond doubt to be *the* answer.

As a highly-successful, politically-conscious businessman— the first to come forward with really substantial financial support for the movement—was later to say: "The proper foundation for representative governments must be representative elections ... But *All Party Alliance* is the stroke of genius which would complete the reform of government in a way which proportional representation alone could not."

One of the greatest advantages of *All Party Alliance*, to my own mind, is that it provides Proportional Representation without all the procedural complexities of existing P.R. systems which arouse such suspicion and mistrust in electors accustomed to a straightforward choice between known candidates.

In its political form alone, it provides a blueprint for a parliament which could win the nation's respect—and regain its own. And in its political and industrial forms together, it provides a system of government which could, and I am sure will, set an example in social and political justice for the world to follow.

I had watched bleakly as one political pundit after another bemoaned the parlous state of Britain's economy and related it to the partisan anarchy of our industrial relations, or deplored public 'apathy' over things political and related it to disillusion and the credibility gap: all of them either deliberately or stupefyingly blind to the basic cause of the national malaise, of which both problems were simply the symptoms.

Now I had come upon a man who, having no party or personal axe to grind, had nothing to fear from hauling both problems into the light of day—and relating them to each other. A man who, moreover, having diagnosed the disease with crystal clarity, had set out with single-minded determination to provide the cure.

"There had to be an answer," he says, and the comment is revealing. Because to John Creasey, as his myriad readers could no doubt have told me before I came to recognise it, any problem is simply a solution standing on its head . . .

*And All Party Alliance is so demonstrably the right solution:* In essence, a set of democratic safeguards which will ensure us the true representative government which is already ours by constitutional right but which the parties today deny us.

It is worth reiterating that under *All Party Alliance,* elections will be fought exactly as now: each party seeking public support for its policies and its candidates. There will *not* be 'A.P.A.' candidates and 'non-A.P.A.' candidates. But every candidate will seek election in the knowledge that, if successful, he will serve in a parliament where his right to an effective voice in the nation's affairs will be respected; where he will be safeguarded from party pressures: free to vote *with* his party on every issue before parliament, if he chooses; equally free to vote against it, without penalty, in the interests of his constituents or the nation.

Every elector will be able to vote in the knowledge that, whether or not his own party candidate is successful, every vote will count in the political composition of the nation's government—not merely in the House of Commons. *All Party Alliance,* indeed, will do away forever with the scandal of the 'wasted vote'.

True democracy needs truly effective opposition, and John Creasey's proposals will give us an Opposition which can really act as watchdog of our democratic rights: with the power to *bite*, not merely bark. Moreover, by not only ensuring M.P.s the *right* to be honest denied them today by their leaders, but making it disadvantageous to be anything less, *All Party Alliance* will give us the candour and integrity we *must* be able to rely upon, in those who administer the nation's affairs and who act and speak to the world in all our names.

Most important of all: it will give us, at last, the power to demand that M.P.s put public interest before *any* party—or make way for better men who will.

Politicians of all parties have done their best to prevent the public from learning the truth about our present political system. But all over the country, people are beginning to see—and to be shocked by—the politically unjust and morally indefensible manner in which the nation's affairs are administered today.

They are right to be shocked.

Because under the present system, whichever the government party, it is in office on a minority vote of the electorate.

In Britain today we do not have government by all the people, for all the people. What we have, is government *of* all the people, *by* a minority: literally always a government *against* the people. Worse still, what in fact this gives us is government by powerful inner Cabinet and Party Whip.

Yet whichever party is in office, *we*—the taxpayers—*pay* hundreds of men, no matter how provenly brilliant or invaluably experienced, to sit in futile Opposition: powerless to do more than protest, even at legislation or policies they may know beyond doubt to be against the national interest or the public will.

*We pay* for all the projects, often ruinously costly or disastrously inept, embarked upon by a government the majority of the taxpayers do not want and with whose aims and priorities they do not concur.

*We pay* all those M.P.s who vote to the Whips' commands even against what they deem public interest—*and* those who don't vote at all, when in honesty they would vote in opposition.

*We pay* all those M.P.s who dive away from dinner-tables at the sound of the Division Bell and, having heard no word of the debate which preceded it, dash to the House to vote as their Whips command.

*We pay*, in this press-button age, for all that time spent in shuffling through lobbies to vote: all those head-nodding 'Ay's' and head-shaking 'No's'—while much-needed legislation piles up for *lack* of parliamentary time.

*We pay*, in this age of jet-travel and telephones, for all those lengthy recesses once needed to reach and ride round some far-flung constituency on horseback—while much-needed legislation . . .

Worst of all, *we—the all-party electorate—pay* all those Government Whips to ensure that their party's M.P.s *vote into law* Bills based on political policies already rejected by the majority of the voting public.

The name of the game is *POWER*. And it is played by a handful of cynical party bosses who make their own rules as they go along—then change them in the course of play.

We cannot let it continue.

We cannot leave power in the hands of alternating one-party cabals whose only answer to what they find displeasing is all too often the bully's resort to superior force.

Harsh legislation and peremptory decree are no substitute for sound government. However we may have smiled at the comic genius of the Whitehall wit who named the operation 'Sheepskin', we can only wince at the remembered spectacle of armed British troops descending like wolves on the Anguillan fold.

There may be cause for wry humour, too, in the thought of men who have reached some of the highest offices in the land, setting out to destroy the grammar and public school systems which gave them their start and presumably helped ensure their success. But in a field so essentially controversial as education, there is nothing remotely amusing in the thought of a bunch of blinkered egoists using their purely temporary authority even to try to bulldoze into being a system of education which—no matter what its merits—is basically founded in a policy of dulling diamonds in order to polish stones.

We *must* halt this trend towards the Orwellian nightmare of totalitarian, Big Brother-run everything.

We cannot leave the nation's affairs at the mercy of the kind of unyielding, unteachable, self-righteous bureaucratic mentality which, at national level, can result in a law as calamitously unprescient and awesomely inept as the Land Commission Act—and at local level is too often seen at its chillingly unfeeling worst in the Compulsory Purchase Order, by which a man can be deprived of his home for the price of a secondhand bicycle.

Who, with any pretensions to respect for human rights, was not disgusted by the unsurpassable arrogance of 'the planners' who decided to wipe out the Malvern Hills village of Wyche because it 'spoils the view'? Or stunned by their pompous indignation at the protests of villagers, some of whose great-grandfathers had lived there before them, that in a hundred years this was the first complaint?

"They are being pretty selfish," complained one county councillor. "The people who visit the hills don't want to see places like that."

The people who *live* in the hills *love* their homes. If the mini-power game players don't like them, let them plant trees. In a country whose housing shortage is a national tragedy, any readiness by authority to worsen it is a national disgrace. And there are other houses than Wyche's, on that same council list: "We are not disclosing which ones, because it might cause alarm."

God knows it *should* cause alarm.

As to the propriety of Cabinet Ministers serving on a party's national executive, the question pales into insignificance beside the thought that any member at all of such a tremendously powerful pressure-group dare presume to dictate policy to the nation's government. The only time any party executive will have a *right* to a voice in the nation's government is the day that same right is accorded to *all* the people, *all* the time.

Leaders and spokesmen of all parties have stayed significantly silent in the face of growing and outspoken concern, in some very high places, at the alarming erosion of private freedom and denial of public will in Britain today. And no party, throughout John Creasey's four by-elections, ever tried to refute his blunt accusations that Britain today is moving towards dictatorship.

Indeed, how could they?

Forcing a man by threats and intimidation to vote against his conscience is a very short step from forcing a man by threats and intimidation to give false evidence, or sign a false confession. When the man under pressure is an elected Member of Parliament, required by the constitution to represent *all* his constituents, whatever their parties, then it is time the more articulate among us demanded an end to this flagrant flouting of his—and our own—democratic rights.

Because either we forget about democracy in this country, or we act, urgently, to stop this slide towards dictatorship-by-default. Either the parties do, *or do not,* believe in

# SUMMATION

Democracy demands that the people be consulted, and the obvious way is by referendum. Party politicians have always rejected calls for regular referenda with ponderous talk of expense to the taxpayer, and the allegedly near-insuperable problems of organisation. Yet every party, every M.P., and every national newspaper has long been fully-apprised of John Creasey's brilliantly-simple plan for a National Referendum to be held in conjunction with the annual Council (local government) elections.

*Just one extra ballot-box at each polling-booth, and two ballot-papers instead of one* and the people could have their say every year on every important issue creating public controversy: no extra organisation needed, and the cost would be negligible. If the parties sincerely regretted those stumbling-blocks to democratic justice, why have they not jumped at the chance to implement a system which overcomes them?

Unless the government does have the honesty to ask—and the integrity to respect—what the people want, we cannot hope for the truly representative government which is our right. And rising generations assuredly will not settle for lip-service democracy and rights more honoured in the breach than the observance.

The youth of this television age are vastly better-informed on the justices and injustices of this world than their parents and grandparents before them. Not only have they grown up literally watching history happen: they have grown up watching the instant-historians clash as they interpret the same facts from totally opposing points of view.

The result is a healthy rejection by young people generally of bigotry and intolerance in any sphere, above all in religion, race and politics: a flat refusal to accept that total right must necessarily lie with any one group of people or set of beliefs, however sincerely held. Nor have the educative effects of television been confined to the young.

Indeed, what the party pundits don't seem to realise is that Jingoism and the whitewash bucket went out when programmes like *What The Papers Say* came in. People, who before the advent of the factual broadcast never saw a newspaper or heard any party viewpoint save their own, were suddenly seeing and hearing the lot—with all the sins of political bias made unequivocally plain.

And true comparisons beget true standards. It is no longer possible to manipulate mass opinion or evoke unquestioning, and unearned, loyalty by deliberately fostering the 'Them *versus* Us' approach to social and industrial relations, which has so long divided the nation.

The people today have had enough of the power-game. They want something different—something better. Quite simply, they want a government they can all respect; national leaders they can trust, national goals they deem worth working for, national policies they can be proud of.

Politicians who blame poor turn-outs at the polls on 'public apathy' are simply burying their heads in the sand.

I am one of those abstaining millions—and it is certainly not apathy which keeps me from voting. Nor is there anything apathetic about the degree of distrust and suspicion towards the present political system, which I so constantly encounter. In a great many cases, certainly, the refusal to vote stems from nothing more than a resentfully-arrived at conviction that however they vote, 'it won't help'. But among a very large and increasing proportion it is simply a refusal to take further part in an electoral process which is not only an exercise in futility but a travesty of justice.

*The wonder is not that so many abstain, but that so many still vote.*

The enforced subjection to one-party rule and absence of political choice epitomised in Communist and Fascist regimes is totally repugnant to democratic minds. Yet in Britain today, we are permanently subjected to one-party rule, and the hollowness of our political choice is grimly evident in the mockery of parliamentary by-elections in which the real winner can only be the ruling party.

All the sweeping Conservative victories of the last three years achieved, was to swell the ranks of the powerless Opposition. None of the winning candidates' supporters gained a voice in the government or policies of the nation: that privilege was reserved for the so-called losers. Labour successes over the same period were equally empty: they simply swelled the ranks of Whip-controlled government back-benchers. Minority party winners, of course, could not even offer their supporters a voice in the *next* government.

Of all the hundreds of thousands of party supporters who went to the polls between 1966 and 1969, only those who voted *for* the regime got the government of their choice—and they would still have had it, if they had all stayed home. *In other words, not one vote cast in a score or more parliamentary by-elections made one iota of difference to the actual balance of power, or to the national and international policies pursued by a minority-elected government in ALL our names.*

And exactly the same would have been true with the Conservative Party in power and the Labour Party in

Opposition.

The only electors who did manage to make their votes serve a truly democratic purpose, in recent years, were those who used them to declare their rejection of one-party rule and their support for *All Party Alliance*: those thousands of thoughtful men and women in Nuneaton and Brierley Hill, Gorton and Oldham, who cared enough for their country and their fellow-men to forget personal advantage and past political allegiances and back John Creasey's call for a voice for *all* the people, *all* the time, in a government which puts the nation's interests before *any* party's.

But until enough of the electorate follow their lead in demanding true representative government, the meaningless farce of empty victories and tongue-in-cheek defeats will be re-enacted at every by-election. And more than half even of those who bother to vote, will be virtually disenfranchised at every General Election.

To dismiss public revulsion from that state of affairs as 'apathy' is to insult the intelligence of a serious-minded electorate.

How blind, do the parties suppose, must electors *be*, before they wake to the fact that a party with more votes cast against it than for it can steam-roller its partisan policies through Parliament, unprevented *and unpreventable*?

How often, do the parties suppose, must electors *hear* winning candidates pay lip-service to their constitutional duty to represent *all* their constituents—only to go straight off to vote as per party command?

How much, do the parties suppose, will the electors *take,* before they all turn in disgust from those who uphold a system which penalises honesty, puts party advantage before public interest, and parades as the democracy it so effectively strangles?

How long, do the parties suppose, will the electors *wait,* before they demand their right to a voice at all times in the policies pursued by their government in *all* their names—and for which they *all* have to foot the bill?

The man who pays the piper has the right to call the tune. When that economic fact of life is backed by dormant but *existing* constitutional right, the politicians ignore it at their peril.

Not that blindness to the economic facts of life is confined to the politician. It has long been obvious that the superfluity of Trade Unions in Britain must, in the name of common sense, give way eventually to some more practical form of worker-representation. Both work-force and management need rescuing from the archaic and unpardonably time-wasting processes of negotiation to which they are subject today.

And certainly, calls upon trade loyalty as justification for disruptive action in unrelated industries, with all the chain-reaction economic hardship that entails, are no more morally-tenable than calls to one-party loyalty, at the expense of all others. Both epitomise the 'I'm all right, Jack' mentality which totally ignores the responsibility, in an unavoidably interdependent society, of each man to his fellows. And the bitter wrangling between blindly self-interested Unions is one of the major causes of industrial unrest.

The *need* for reform is not in doubt. But never, till now, has anyone provided the Unions with a demonstrably valid *reason* to change.

John Creasey's *Alliance in Industry* not only provides that reason: it also provides such demonstrably beneficial incentives that a refusal to change must surely, to sound minds, be unthinkable.

# EVOLUTION TO DEMOCRACY

It is no use hoping that without really radical reform, the problems besetting industry today can ever be cured. Nothing will win the socialist/nationalisers and the capitalist/private enterprisers to the opposing view. But so long as each 'side' accepts democracy as a basic British right, neither can, in justice, cavil at a solution which makes equal concessions to both. And *Alliance in Industry* does just that.

Certainly, industrial strike will not be ended while basic cause for unrest exists. When it comes down to hard facts of wasted man-hours, reduced production, delayed deliveries and broken contracts, whether a particular strike is sparked off by a political agitator, a misguided hot-head or a power-obsessed shop steward, is of singular indifference. What matters is that the stoked-up resentment and distrust exist: a permanent powder-keg only needing that spark.

It is no use telling the man at the bench or on the factory floor that continually-increasing productivity is the only way to a better, brighter, more prosperous society. Ingrained suspicion excusably demands: prosperous for whom? On past form, what reason has he for faith that present plans and promises will not end in future fiasco—and another Slump?

What he needs are demonstrably worthwhile incentives: good reason to trust, good reason for hope, tangible proof that his own vital importance to the nation's well-being is truly appreciated—that *his* well-being, *his* prosperity, are of genuine concern to those who exhort him to greater effort.

*Alliance in Industry* provides those incentives, that proof of appreciation, in the form of truly worthwhile rewards—and a financial stake in his own future.

It would be hard to overstate the value and importance of these proposals—because strikes and restrictive practices certainly will not be ended by legislation. We cannot gaol the entire labour-force of Britain, nor even that of any Union. Nor, in the unhappy event that we could, would it be any answer: no man labouring under a sense of grievance is capable of putting his best into his job. And while no free society can function successfully unless its members exercise their rights with responsibility, the right to withhold his labour must in the name of human dignity remain the prerogative of every man.

The only true solution of the problem, therefore, would be one which can put an end to industrial strife while completely safeguarding the fundamental right of the individual worker.

*Alliance in Industry* provides the solution—by preserving the *right* to strike, but removing the *cause*.

The proposals contained in *All Party Alliance* and *Alliance in Industry* have from their inception been freely available to any and all parties, and over the past three years several M.P.s and even one or two Ministers have availed themselves of this open invitation, to publicly put their own names to specific aspects of the proposed reforms they personally most approved.

Indeed, there could be few better illustrations of the difference of approach which divides the public-spirited from the power-minded. Because nothing would gratify John Creasey more—and nothing, in my own opinion, could benefit the country more—than to see *all* M.P.s adopt his policies as their own. Whereas politicians of all parties unashamedly admit to guarding with the utmost secrecy, when not in power, any policies or plans they evolve for the more efficient or more equitable conduct of the nation's affairs.

"Why should we tell the government our ideas?" is the common argument, from men whose parties may be years away from office: "They'll only use them themselves and take all the credit."

The attitude of men like John Creasey could be summed up as: the time to throw a life-belt is when the swimmer is struggling—not after he drowns. And so long as the nation gets the benefit, what matter who gets the credit?

But the 'Them *versus* Us' approach which the present system fosters has become such ingrained habit in politics today that even the most respected and sincere of party politicians will accept the 'rules' of this appalling power-game without even thinking to question their morality.

As Harold Macmillan wrote, in his *Tides of Fortune*: "Great political parties, like championship boxers, need a respite after one fight before they re-enter the ring, partly to recoup their strength, partly to collect sufficient financial backers for another contest."

No attempt to *disguise* this entirely partisan approach to the business of government. No comprehension of how shockingly cynical this attitude must seem, to anyone not steeped in the cold philosophy of political double-think. No apology to those millions who had voted for his (losing) party and, because of the system it chooses to help maintain, were thereby virtually dis-enfranchised. And obviously, no faintest awareness of the question which as obviously screams to be asked: *"Meanwhile, what of the nation?"*

How can any party which even half-believes its own constantly-reiterated claims that its opponents will seriously damage the economy, or cause hardship or loss to *any* section of the population, dare to claim that it cares for the nation's well-being, or for individual rights—while flagrantly ignoring both, for its own advantage?

But by making total power the all-important goal, the present system makes this frighteningly short-sighted team *versus* team approach inevitable. No party can be certain of seeing even the most nationally desirable of its policies put into practice *except* by gaining power, so the prime concern of the government party is always to stay in office, and the prime concern of the Opposition to get it out. The obsession of each party with this totally self-imposed need for absolute supremacy not only blinds them to their duty to put the nation's interests first, but blinds them even to the advisability of making their inexcusable self-interest less offensively plain.

As John Creasey says: "It is as if we were to tell our World Cup team: 'Look, we're competing with the rest of the world, and you've been picked to represent us because you're judged to be the best men for the job. Now, here's how we'll play it: five of you (the Tories) shoot into *that* goal, and five (Labour) into the other, while you (the Liberal) just kick anywhere you like.' It is madness! If we, as a nation, can't work as a team, how can anyone win—except our competitors?"

It *is* madness. It is also shameful and unforgiveable irresponsibility. And there is absolutely no reason or justification for its continuance. If the politicians could previously claim that they were helpless—that there was no way to beat 'the system'—they cannot take refuge in that excuse now. John Creasey has shown them the way to rostore and maintain their own *and* the people's democratic rights.

Party hard-liners, unable to fault his proposals or the principles he advocates, have called them and him, everything from 'Fascist' to 'Communist'—two calumnies which neatly cancel each other out. Others have tried to dismiss them, and him, as 'too idealistic'.

If it is idealistic to want, and to fight for, a fairer deal, a better chance, a brighter future for one's fellow-men—then yes: John Creasey is an idealist. But there can be few greater *realists* than this highly-successful, internationally-renowned, entirely self-made man. And it is to just such realistic idealists—to men with their feet on the ground and their eyes on the brighter, better, juster horizons—that mankind owes its progress.

To quote the Duke of Edinburgh: "I always felt that the world is made up of two kinds of people. The majority are those who are perfectly content to let everything go along as before. Then there is the very small minority who are prepared to say: 'Stop! This is the wrong way to do it! We're going *that* way!' And these are the people who really make history. These are the people who set the world along a new course."

It is surely only realistic to refuse to subscribe to any course of human progress which will *not* lead with absolute inevitability to a society acceptable to all. Indeed, how in sanity can anyone think anything less than the best worth striving for?

When John Creasey first called for this, coalition-plus, of the best men the nation could provide, to get the country out—and keep it out—of the mess into which successive one-party governments had led it, his was a lone voice, crying in the wilderness. Within a few short months, thoughtful men in every walk of life had begun to echo his plea. But as one by-election after another reflected an obviously wider public concern at the state of the nation, those with a vested interest in gagging the present system's critics became more and more determinedly active.

Increasingly, throughout his own four by-elections, political correspondents who had grown convinced that his proposals really were the answer 'if the parties will only admit it', reported to us in disgust and anger at the refusal of their various national and (with some heartening exceptions) major provincial newspaper editors to print what they wrote about *All Party Alliance*.

After the declaration of the poll at the Oldham West by-election (his fourth), T.V. commentators were unanimous in their surprise at 'the astonishingly large vote for John Creasey'.

And indeed, for an Independent candidate (with only a one-woman 'political machine'—me!—in place of all the resources of solidly-established national and local organisations at the party candidates' disposal) to win 13.2% of the total votes cast in an abysmally low poll, is in itself a minor miracle. But when compared with the number of votes which, despite their most strenuous efforts (and the rallying speeches of every party's 'big guns') were all those mammoth party machines could grind out, in an area where each had its own long-entrenched traditional support, the proportion is even more remarkable: one to every three and a half Conservatives; two to every five Socialists; *two to every one Liberal.*

Yet next morning and in the days that followed, just four out of eight national newspapers even referred editorially to this historically unique and highly significant result. Even then, two (the *Daily Sketch* and *The Guardian*) did so only in the context of its effect upon Liberal expectations; not the truly remarkable success of a new political movement which offered a viable alternative to our present patently-discredited system of government.

*The Times* alone reported with factual impartiality. As that highly-respected political commentator, John Chartres, wrote: "The most significant aspects of the Oldham West result were not that Mr. Bruce Campbell, the Conservative candidate, won, but that only just over half the electorate turned out to vote and that Mr. John Creasey achieved a substantial 3,389 votes and came third."

The *Daily Telegraph*, which throughout the campaign had ignored both the Liberal and John Creasey—reporting as if it were a straight fight between Labour and Conservatives— actually mentioned the Liberal (who lost his deposit) in its report of the poll, but omitted any reference to *All Party Alliance* even in the formal statement of result.

These obviously calculated omissions were of course as obviously intended to deaden the impact of his vote and play down the strengthening appeal of *All Party Alliance*. And as a journalist to whom 'comment is free; facts are sacred', I found this partisan-inspired press censorship truly alarming. Because in essence, it is an all-too-successful attempt to stifle the voice of truth. It is tantamount to saying: "Let us silence the voice of the man who says what we do not wish the people to hear."

Coming as it did so soon after the swift dismissal of I.P.C. chairman Cecil King, who had dared to call publicly for some form of coalition government and plainly intended using the *Mirror* to test public opinion, this political gagging seemed doubly sinister. Moreover, the total black-out of all radio and television comment on John Creasey and *All Party Alliance*, from that time on, despite the eager enthusiasm of many of the networks' reporters and staff, left me more deeply perturbed than ever that both the I.T.A. and (in flat contradiction to the recommendations of the 1952 Commission) the B.B.C. should be headed by party political appointees.

The very scale of the power and influence behind this obvious 'conspiracy of silence' would have daunted any lesser man and was doubtless intended and expected to daunt John Creasey. But: "I had to give up," he says, of another point at which most men would assuredly have done just that, "or change my method of attack."

And John Creasey does not give up . . .

A polio victim at the age of two, medical experts prophesied that he would never walk. Aware of just what that meant, at the age of four, *he* prophesied that he would. At the age of six, he walked to school . . .

At the age of ten, his headmaster (deeply impressed by an essay he wrote on 'An imaginary conversation between Marshal Foch and the Kaiser') told him he might well one day earn a living at writing. Between the age of ten and seventeen, assured on all sides that he never would, and despite a crushing 743 rejection slips, he never stopped trying. *(How many men, let alone boys, would have had the courage to try, 743 times?)*

"Write about the things you know," the pundits always advised, and accordingly, he had always done so. But at the age of seventeen, "never having been in love, or out of England."—he wrote a love story about a Chinese girl and a Japanese boy in the mountains of Tibet—and he was 'in business'.

('I had to give up, or change my method of attack',)

At twenty-six, he faced the fact that he could not keep a family on the proceeds of the two books a year that were the limit publishers considered saleable by any one author. So he simply started writing two books a year under a *variety* of names.

('I had to give up, or . . . ')

At forty, with two hundred books published in England but unable to sell in the U.S.A., he went there to ask why. Nineteen publishers and editors told him he never would be able to sell in the U.S.A.—and each gave him a different reason. But: 'There had to be one basic reason' and the man who will not take 'no' for an answer finally worked it out:

# EVOLUTION TO DEMOCRACY

('The English read objectively; the Americans, subjectively')—
and again, he was 'in business'.

('I had to give up, or . . . ')

Today, he has had nearly 200 books published in the
U.S.A. and now averages 20 new titles published there
annually. And earlier this year, in the country where his
writings were never going to succeed, he was awarded the
Grand Mastership of the Mystery Writers of America—an
honour never before bestowed upon a non-American.

Today, indeed, the boy who tried and tried and tried again,
has written more books than any other author living (532 at
last count) and sees them regularly translated into twenty-five
languages and sold in over a hundred countries around the
world . . .

Those who would seek to silence him, should take heed:
*when John Creasey sets himself a goal, experience proves that
its achievement is simply a matter of time.* And since justice is
his abiding passion, and the chance for people to live together
in confident harmony the greatest of all his life's ambitions,
the actuality of *All Party Alliance* government is not a
question of 'if'—simply of 'when'.

If those vested interests can bar him from the listening,
viewing, and national press reading public, they cannot gag
him in the field where he has his own ready-made and
constantly-increasing 'audience' of millions. So, once more, he
has 'changed his method of attack'—and this book is the result.

I am completely convinced that once it is widely available,
once the proposals *and* the urgent need for such reform
become known throughout the country, the plain common
sense of the voting public will do the rest. In war, after all, we
would not dream of allowing one party to decide the nation's
fate. We know that to win, we must have the best government

the country can provide: the best man for the job, in every job, regardless of party. Why settle for anything less than the best, in peace?

In the past year or so, several of the more influential provincial newspapers, particularly in the industrial north, have shown increasingly serious interest in both the political and industrial reforms John Creasey advocates. I have no doubt that others will follow their lead, in the months ahead: that eventually pressure of public opinion will force the national press to follow suit. And that pressure of public opinion will also, very soon, force the parties to see their duty to take the first essential step to true democracy in Britain by restoring true political justice to the people.

Once we have government by *All Party Alliance,* I believe that *Alliance in Industry* will inevitably follow. Because nothing approaching its absolute justice, absolute common sense and demonstrable benefit to the whole nation has been put forward by any party, by the government, by the Trade Unions or by Big Business, in solution of our economic and industrial ills.

For *three years,* before Mrs. Barbara Castle produced her highly-controversial "In Place of Strife"—or Sir Paul Chambers produced his plan to reduce income tax, in five years' time, by 2/3d in the pound—we had been urging on both of them (as on every M.P., every leading industrialist) this blue-print for industrial unity and national prosperity which, *if in operation today,* could reduce income tax by 3/-d in the pound.

All manner of economic and other experts have tried, but none has been able, to fault the absolute justice and practicability of either *All Party Alliance,* or *Alliance in Industry.* And to all who, when they have read the proposals, also recognise their absolute justice and practicability, I can only say:

Ask yourself WHY no party, WHY no M.P., WHY no Trade Union, WHY no national newspaper has been prepared to pass them on to you, the tax-paying public, for YOUR consideration?

If I was alarmed at the state of this country three years ago, the insidious pressures and power-politics that have gone to the gagging of one man who dared to try to set it right have left me appalled. And perhaps now all those friends and relatives the world over, who for three years have fretted and fumed over *why* I allow myself to be 'buried away in the wilds'—sacrificing my own career to advance another author's', etc. etc., will finally understand.

Because, 'John Creasey, author' needs no advancing. But John Creasey, author of this brilliant blue-print for a political and industrial evolution that I am convinced will go down in history as a landmark in Britain's progress to true democracy, needs and deserves for his brain-child all the 'advancing' it can get.

All reform, after all, *starts* with one man. But someone has to be the first to listen. Someone has to care enough to help. Someone has to start the snowball of support that will become the avalanche that bursts the barriers of bigotry and self-interest, to force that reform into being.

That snowball has been started, and is growing splendidly as it gathers speed. It is not a question of 'if'—simply of *'when'*. And for the chance to help ensure true representative government in Britain for generations to come, three years seems a minor price to pay.

*Olga Stringfellow*

# NOTES